Break the Mold

Step into Your Full Potential in Christ

Cody A. Wallace

Break The Mold

Break the Mold: Step into Your Full Potential in Christ

©2021 Grace Acres Press

Published by Grace Acres Press
Independence, Missouri

Edited by Chelle Annete Islas and Catherine Cone
Cover design by Abbie Boyd

ISBN – 978-1-60265-079-4

All Scripture quotations, except those noted otherwise are from the New American Standard Bible, ©1960, 1962, 1963, 1968, 1971, 1972, 1973, 1975, 1977, and 1995 by the Lockman Foundation.

Believing in Jesus Christ as Savior is not the end of the journey, but just the beginning. On that journey the believer will soon encounter and be challenged by Romans 12:1-2 to be a living sacrifice. Cody Wallace has done a masterful job of unpacking the meaning and significance of these verses in a way that will help the believer grow. His insights come from a knowledge of the biblical text, the original language, and his life and ministry experiences. The reader will find an easy enjoyable style and flow in the book, but more importantly, the motivation to commit to the Lord in a deeper way. Christians should read, digest, and use this book to help others on their journey.

–**Charles C. Bing**, ThM, PhD
Founder and president, GraceLife Ministries

If you are sincerely desiring to live above the fray during these most divisive times that we are living in, then I highly recommend you read *Break the Mold: Step into Your Full Potential in Christ*. Pastor Cody Wallace, in this short, easy to read book, helps us navigate through those things that keep us from being obedient to the gospel, conforming to the "patterns of this present world." He gives us insight on how to abandon selfish ambitions within our respective ministries, working collaboratively with other Christ followers, and ultimately giving God the glory for all the great things He does with and through our lives.

–**Al Fernandez**
Regional representative, SBC

Too many Christians assume that believing in Jesus is synonymous with following Him. Pastor Cody Wallace says in his book, "You might believe in Jesus, but that doesn't mean you follow Him." I have known and served under Pastor Wallace in the local church for many years, and I know personally that his passion is to see Christians transformed into the image of Christ by following Him. This book will let you see Romans 12:1-2 in a different transformable way. So if you are seeking transformation in your Christian walk, this book is for you!

–John Echeverria
Associate Pastor, Southwest Community Church

An inspired and powerful book by Cody Wallace. This book is encouraging, challenging, and has massive power to unleash your potential in Christ. Cody's words are biblical, and his wisdom will inspire readers to break the mold of this world and abide in Christ.

–Joe Filer
Founder & Director of Freedom Church Movement
Author of *Reproducing Grace: Starting a Free Grace Movement in Your Region*

Cody argues good reasoning from Scripture and gives very encouraging metaphors for readers to understand how to apply God's truths to their lives. Reading Cody's book will help you grow a closer relationship with Jesus and accomplish your life mission.

–Rod Earls, PhD, DMin
Professor of Practical Studies
John W. Rawlings School of Divinity

In these powerful pages, Pastor Cody Wallace leads you on a journey that takes you from merely believing in Jesus, to following Jesus, and then to being transformed into his image. If you desire to find new purpose, clear direction, and significant meaning in your life—buckle up!

–Rick Blackwood, DD, DMin, EdD
Leading from the Pulpit

Way to many Christians are indiscernible from the world around them. They are conforming to the world, not transforming into the image of Christ. That is why I am so excited about Cody Wallace's book *Break the Mold*! Cody interweaves interesting personal stories with relevant Scriptural truths to encourage us to achieve all that God desires for our lives.

–Jim Scudder
Pastor, Quentin Road Baptist
President, Dayspring Bible College

Break the Mold by Cody Wallace is a book that accomplishes a rare feat. It is both brief and deep. *Break the Mold* provides the reader with an in-depth look at how to dive deeper into the Christian faith while sitting at easily digestible length for the young Christian. If you have yet to step forward on your Christian journey down the road to greater things in Christ, *Break the Mold* is a wonderful place to start.

–Shawn Willson
Pastor of Grace Community Bible Church, River Ridge, LA
Rev Reads Book Reviews

Cody argues good reasoning from Scripture and gives very encouraging metaphors for readers to understand how to apply God's truths to their lives.

Reading Cody's book will help you grow a closer relationship with Jesus and accomplish your life mission.

You will enjoy this book!

–Rod Earls, PhD, DMin
Online Assistant Professor of Practical Studies
John W. Rawlings School of Divinity

How do caterpillars become beautiful butterflies? The secret found in nature provides a living metaphor for the process God takes His followers through to the place of true transformation.

Dear friend and pastor, Cody Wallace, unpacks an insightful process to our own metamorphosis as followers of Jesus toward ever more glory and lives transformed into new and vibrant creations in Jesus. Looking into the words in just two verses in Romans 12:1-2, our author unpacks the riches and mines the depths as both scholar with careful etymological study and as pastor, expressing pastoral concerns bringing the richest to light and life to be lived out by believers.

If you are a veteran pastor in the teaching ministry of the word, you will benefit from Cody's deep word studies. If you are leading a Bible study and concerned about bringing these truths to bear upon those you lead, the practical insights will stimulate you into pathways to bless your study.

If you wonder, does this author live the truths he professes and writes about with such passion and clarity? Our friend is the real deal. As a son, husband, dad, pastor, educator, author, local church man, he lives out the talk and walks the talk. The truths taught are the same truths lived. Just ask his dear wife and kids. They get to see him up close and personal day in and day out. And an added bonus, Cody lives these truths out and teaches them in one of the great cities of America, Miami. These truths, modeled for Miami, apply to every culture the world over.

So, I suggest you begin with an open Bible, notepad, and cup of coffee and slowly work your way through his study and allow God to bring deeper transformation to your heart as well. Soar and fly like the beautiful butterfly God has made you to be.

–Dr. Jim O'Neill
Co-founder and President of NextGen Leaders Conference
Director of Mobilization, Frontier Ventures

Your theology of discipleship will be an extension of your theology of salvation. If you believe in salvation by works, you will see discipleship as part of the effort to work your way into heaven. Sadly, that view has been popular throughout history- and it is the formula for guilt, disappointment, and burnout. By contrast, Cody Wallace "breaks the mold" by seeing discipleship as an extension of the precious truth that salvation is by grace through faith, apart from works. Far from encouraging laziness, the rich soil of grace provides the best environment for producing a fruitful life of service to Christ. Wallace presents every reader with this challenge: after you believe in Jesus, will you also choose to follow Him? If you do, what you can gain is incomparably greater than what you might lose.

–Shawn Lazar
Grace in Focus Radio

Break The Mold

There are many people that have fed into this book and my life, and for that I thank all of you. This book is dedicated to my lovely wife Margret, "Meg." The Lord has blessed me with you and "broke the mold" after creating you. To my kids, parents, and brothers and sisters. . . thank you all for helping me see Scripture in every story in life.

Break The Mold

Foreword

Many people today confuse entering the Christian life with living it. They even make whether or not one *looks like* a Christian a test of whether or not they *are* a Christian.

Cody Wallace doesn't do that. He recognizes that eternal salvation is God's free gift bought and paid for by His Son's death on the cross and His resurrection the third day with no strings attached. What Cody *does* do is encourage us to take the Christian life seriously.

Therefore, this book is for believers, not unbelievers. Diving into Romans 12:1-2, Cody encourages us to live the kind of sacrificial life that may take us out of our comfort zones but makes a difference in a world that needs to see Christlike living. One sentence contained in this book summarizes his heart: "We need to reject the temptation to cling to comfort and instead embrace growth."

As you read this book you will sense the passion behind Cody's words–the same passion I have seen in him from the time I met him years ago. This book is not written to give information; it is written to change lives. There is not one believer who would not be challenged and helped by what Cody has to say.

You will come away from this book not only knowing the direction that believers ought to go, but you will also learn how to get there. As Cody readily admits, there will be costs and sacrifices along the way, but there is tremendous reward at the end of the trail.

R. Larry Moyer
Founder and CEO
EvanTell

Break The Mold

Preface

The writing of this book has been a real personal journey for me. Although the manuscript was written over a few years in short stints during seminary, it has been in development for twenty plus years. So why write about such a small passage?

When I was ten, I learned about Jesus and how He died, was buried, and rose again so I could go to heaven. I grew up in a "Christian" home, and it seemed as if the doctor said, "Congratulations! You have given birth to a healthy Christian boy!" at my birth. For years I felt that because my parents were believers that meant I was. But on Easter Sunday 1992, I learned the truth. Ephesians 2:8 and 9 says, "For by grace you have been saved through faith; and that not of yourselves, it is the gift of God; not as a result of works, so that no one may boast." No one could earn heaven, no one could buy it, and it wasn't up to anyone to get it for me.

"Truly, truly, I say unto you, he who believes has eternal life" (John 6:47). As this verse says, it was up to me to believe what Jesus did. So, that Easter Sunday during Sunday school I trusted Jesus as my Savior.

I want to tell you that from then on, I lived for the Lord and had a relationship with Him, but that would be a lie. I had a rocky relationship with God after that, and for the next eight years, my walk was shaky at best.

In middle school, athletics kept me focused and from rebelling. In high school, I got in trouble with the law because of poor decisions and hanging out with the wrong crowd, but fear of prison hardened my heart and overwhelmed my thoughts to where working out and wrestling became my life.

During one wrestling match, I dislocated my shoulder, and tore my labrum in three spots, stretching out tendons, muscles, and ligaments. I never got to wrestle in states or nationals, and my hopes and dreams of athletics beyond high school came crashing down. I lost my car because I could no longer drive a stick shift. I lost my friends because I was not a wrestler anymore and had no car.

When I graduated, I got very depressed and moved to Orlando where I started to drink and smoke pot every day to try to bury the memories. Three months before my twentieth birthday I woke up crying. I was upset, alone, and confused. What was the meaning of my life? I felt empty, lost, and meaningless. For some reason, I looked at my bookshelf, and I saw my dusty old Bible I had not opened in years. I grabbed ahold of it and opened it, and the verse it opened up to grabbed hold of me.

> Therefore I urge you, brethren, by the mercies of God, to present your bodies a living and holy sacrifice, acceptable to God, which is your spiritual service of worship. *2* And do not be conformed to this world, but be transformed by the renewing of your mind, so that you may prove what the will of God is, that which is good and acceptable and perfect (Romans 12:1-2).

Jesus wanted me! He wanted a relationship with me! He wanted me to give my life to Him and be guided by Him—that is the meaning for life! When you hand your life to Jesus and say, I am here for you and only you, that is the first step. It is being a living sacrifice, meaning doing the things He would do, putting others first, loving all, and living an example. It is committing to follow Him. It's about living your life as a paradox; I am dying to myself, my selfish thoughts and wants so that I can live, putting others and God first. My hope is that the study of this passage consumes your heart, mind, and actions like it did for me.

"And He was saying to them all, 'If anyone wishes to come after Me, he must deny himself, and take up his cross daily and follow Me'" (Luke 9:23). You might believe in Jesus, but that doesn't mean you follow Jesus. The passage states, to follow

Jesus, you must deny yourself, take up your cross live for Jesus. I had never given myself up; I had never let go of my life. I prayed to God and begged Him to forgive me for walking away from Him, and like the prodigal son in Luke 15, Jesus took me back in.

Romans 12:1-2 has consumed my life, it has breathed life anew into me, and it has become my mission to live out. You may think that it is too late for you. You may think that God doesn't want you like you are. But if God can use a sinner like me, He can use a sinner like you. My life view has changed; I live for Christ, not passions, desire, and the world's approval. The Lord has blessed my life with a loving wife, three children and a church family. . . .but above all I have purpose, direction, and meaning. Jesus wants me. "Come to Me, all who are weary and heavy-laden, and I will give you rest" (Matthew 11:28).

Jesus wants you just the way you are. As 2 Corinthians 12:9 says His grace is perfected in weakness; that is why I share my weakness, my stories, and my passion for how Romans 12:1-2 has changed my outlook on life. I hope this serves as a challenge to all believers to grow in their relationship with Jesus, and walk as a follower of His.

Break The Mold

Table of Contents

Break The Mold

Chapter One

HOW CAN I BE A LIVING SACRIFICE?

Therefore I urge you, brethren, by the mercies of God, to present your bodies as a living and holy sacrifice, acceptable to God, which is your spiritual service of worship. And do not be conformed to this world, but be transformed by the renewing of your mind, so that you may prove what the will of God is, that which is good and acceptable and perfect (Romans 12:1-2).

Are you at the point in your life where you want to take your Spiritual growth to the next level? The problem for many believers is that their desire does not translate to action. Despite their desire to go deeper, instead they keep crawling off the altar! You see, that is the problem with living sacrifices, we must choose whether or not we will make the sacrifice.

Sooner or later, each believer needs to make the decision for themselves. We each will have to answer these essential questions: Do I long to grow my relationship with Christ? Or, am I willing to stagnate to the point of relationship death? The apostle Peter gives us an illustration of how we can deepen our faith, writing "Like newborn babies, long for the pure milk of the word, so that by it you may grow in respect to salvation, if you have tasted the kindness of the Lord" (1 Peter 2:2-3).

The word of God for a new believer is like milk for a newborn baby; it nurtures healthy growth and development. As babies, we drink milk as nourishment. However, had we continued to rely solely on milk, we would not have flourished. This nutritional limitation would stunt physical growth and diminish brain development; a diet of milk alone is inadequate to support a baby's growth.

Similarly, while at first essential, the "pure milk of the word" on its own is insufficient to support a maturing Christian believer. Just as babies are weaned, so too must we as maturing believers wean ourselves from milk and transition to the solid food of God's word as we mature in our faith and grow our relationship with Christ.

Why is it important to take the next step in your faith? The apostle Paul describes the maturation of faith, stating, "When I was a child, I used to speak like a child, think like a child, reason like a child; when I became a man, I did away with childish things" (1 Corinthians 13:11).

An important part of spiritual growth is learning discernment and gaining wisdom. This is a process not unlike the catapiller's transformation into a butterfly. Caterpillars spend their lifetime eating and shedding so growth can occur. Ultimately, each one's purpose is to reach growth that transforms them into a butterfly. Similarly, a maturing believer has the goal of "shedding" the fleshly or worldly mindset and transforming to become more like Christ. As children, we think about only one thing – ourselves; the world revolves around us and our own needs. Our concerns are, I want food, I want attention, and our focus is on self, I want! I want! I want! Me! Me! Me!

However, as we grow in the Lord, our reasoning changes from this type of self-serving and self-centered thought to a more outward-facing, others-serving focus, and this only becomes more true as we seek to have increasingly greater impact for Christ. As maturing Christians, we must grow to think beyond ourselves and our immediate circle. As Paul relates, "As a child, I reasoned like a child," but if we are to mature as believers, it is time we "did away with childish things" in order to broaden our lens and see the bigger picture.

What is the bigger picture? The bigger picture is that we are the body of Christ. We must be living in peace together, loving one another, and working together for His glory. If we do our part by encouraging and loving one another, then we will abandon selfish ambitions in our ministry and instead concern ourselves with reaching others for Christ. Mature believers want to know how to help and how to reach others. When we see the bigger picture we recognize that God is the center of our life and our relationship with Jesus is what matters most. Seeing the bigger picture means looking at the world through God's eyes.

Peter writes, "The Lord is not slow about His promise, as some count slowness, but is patient toward you, not wishing for any to perish but for all to come to repentance" (2 Peter 3:9). God does not wish for any to perish; maturity is opening your eyes to others and having God's heart for their salvation. So how do we start maturing? First, we wean from the beginner's "milk" and move on to the "solid food" that requires us to get in there and chew!

Being a living sacrifice means learning to give back. It means getting into the kind of transformational cocoon that can only be accomplished through the renewing of our minds that comes from reading and studying God's word, and then applying it in our lives. That transformation is worth the effort; it's worth fighting for as Paul explains when he writes, "Fight the good fight of faith; take hold of the eternal life to which you were called and you made the good confession in the presence of many witnesses" (1 Timothy 6:12).

One of the biggest issues we have as believers is that we are not fighting the good fight. The Greek word *kalon* sounds like the English cologne, the fragrant perfume a man wears. You can fight for what has intrinsic value, what is right, what is an up-worthy and righteous call, you can fight for things that have a fragrant aroma, a good pleasing smell, taste, view, and pallet. *Kalon* identifies the "good" while the Greek word *agōnizou* (ἀγωνίζου) is used in the original text to describe the fight itself. This word for "fight" is the source of the English word agonize. This differentiates both the purpose of the fight and the extent of it. We can fight for what has eternal value, what has impact to the Kingdom, or we can be caught up in fighting for temporary things of the day or of this life.

It is easy to get caught up in the fight for a parking spot, or whose turn it is to do the dishes, but this is not the kalēn fight that we, as believers, are called to take up. Furthermore, when we take up the fight, to what extent do we enter into battle? Are we *agonizing* in it? The Christian life is a fight worth engaging. In Ephesians 6:12, Paul clarifies that we don't fight human enemies, we fight the power of the devil, and we do so both for reaching others for Christ and through the power of Christ.

In Chapter 7 of the book of Romans, Paul examines our struggle between the desire to battle what is right in God's eyes and the all-too-human desire of the flesh to do what makes us "happy." This is not the only struggle we face as believers, however. John 17 and Romans 12 both discuss the human struggle against the world and worldliness, the desire to fit in and to conform, the devil's pull on our identity in Christ and the draw to fall into line. We are in a battle, but the one that counts is, as Paul says, the good fight; the one for souls, the one for spiritual growth, the one for the voiceless and the powerless, the fight for the glory of Jesus' name. As believers, we are called to fight this good fight. Paul is saying, struggle to do what is right and to build your faith. Fight, as in *agōnizou* (ἀγωνίζου), with a deep, wrenching, *agonizing* struggle.

We often agonize over things that, if they matter at all, only matter for a brief moment in time. We agonize over long hours we are putting in at work in order to fulfill our desire for a bigger house, a nicer car, or the right social group. People agonize to look the part for people around them and achieve some type of acceptance. These are hardly worth agonizing over when they can only result in obscuring our identity in Christ.

However, if we agonize for the right things, if we struggle toward greater impact for the Lord, if our focus is on heaven and living the word of God, then our focus will be on God and others. This agony will not be misspent and our struggles will not be in vain because we will not be toiling for something that fades away. When a believer approaches the Christian struggle in this manner, they claim victory as described in 2 Timothy 4:7-8: "I have fought the good fight, I have finished the course, I have kept the faith; in the future there is laid up for me the crown of righteousness, which the Lord, the righteous Judge, will award to me on that day; and not only to me, but also to all who have loved His appearing."

This is not the case when we seek the favor of men, however. I recall the day my co-worker and friend was named the employee of the month. As co-workers, all of us celebrated with him because he not only received a certificate and had his picture on the wall, but he also received a $10 gift card, and a one dollar raise to $6.50 an hour. We were all happy for him, but our excitement was short lived; just two weeks later he was fired. It turns out that while we had all been striving to receive the employee of the month award, from that point on none of us wanted anything to do with it!

The fact is that this type of reward quickly fades. We inevitably lose favor in the sight of men, the luster wears off the award, and whatever we thought we achieved is soon forgotten. But with the Lord, the good works of believers are rewarded with an imperishable award. Paul identifies this in 1 Corinthians 9:25 contrasting how the rewards of the world perish and are quickly erased, but the the imperishable crown is for all of eternity. The original Greek, *phtharton* (φθαρτὸν), means "to decay" or "to fall apart," and that is the reward we can expect from the world. The reward for living life for oneself and for the flesh is paid in fading and forgotten currency.

God's reward is imperishable, *aphtharton* (ἄφθαρτον), which means believers' good works will be rewarded with a "superior wreath" which cannot be lost or taken away; it will never decay or fade. In other words, when your life is lived for the Lord, it is never forgotten. When you act for the Lord, it is never without reason. When you speak for the Lord, no word goes out void. This is true because *He* is the One who knows all things, records the truth, notes the victory, and rewards for eternity.

Sadly, in these days, too many Christians are living life with the wrong focus, approaching their Christian life as if this world is all there is and this temporary life is all that matters. Paul warns that this is like boxing with your own shadow; it looks good for a while, but pretty soon everyone realizes you are not willing to get in the real fight. It is like running with no idea which direction to go in. You may get somewhere, but where did you get to, and at what cost? If we live for ourselves we are doing nothing more than boxing with our own shadow. Our lives become an endless race with no course map and no finish line.

Jesus Christ gives us clear direction, stating "Go therefore and make disciples of all the nations, baptizing them in the name of the Father and of the Son and of the Holy Spirit," (Matthew 28:19). The race we are to run is to reach the world with the good news of the gospel, and to disciple others.

Paul reminds us that we are to run the race with our focus on winning (1 Corinthians 9:24). We are to be fit in our training and to remain balanced and in control; our reward in Christ awaits us. Paul understands this because he was a fighter himself. He says it this way, "I have fought the good fight, I have finished the course, I have kept the faith; in the future there is laid up for me the crown of righteousness, which the Lord, the righteous Judge, will award to me on that day; and not only to me, but also to all who have loved His appearing" (2 Timothy 4:7-8).

Paul identifies that he understood the difference between fighting the good fight and fighting a bad one. Fully aware of his impending death, Paul offers a final farewell to Timothy. He communicates that he has no regrets because he used his time in this life wisely, fighting the good fight. Paul goes on to encourage Timothy (and thereby all of us as believers) to fight the right battles and not waste time on the wrong ones. In 2 Timothy 2:14-26, Paul carefully explains the believer's role as a diligent worker, a channel of God, who works as a willing slave under the total command of his master (Jesus Christ).

He doesn't want us walking all of our days in the wrong battles, going toe to toe with someone we love over a dirty spoon, or the color of the wall paint. He admonishes us all to do as he did; go all out in battle for the Glory of the King, and await our crown having hailed His coming. For those of us who walk in faith on this side of eternity, who maintain a heavenly focus while on this earth, our reward is the crown given to us by Jesus Himself. Believers who fight the good fight, who run the race to win, await their crown. Which battle will you fight?

The good fight is defined several times in scripture, including 2 Timothy 2 where Paul defines the good, the bad, the awesome, and the useless. He offers us guidance by delineating that we should do one thing, but not do something else. However, it is Jesus who gives us the the ultimate direction, telling us how to live, make choices, and fight battles. He says, "You are the salt of the earth; but if the salt has become tasteless, how can it be made salty again? It is no longer good for anything, except to be thrown out and trampled under foot by men. You are the light of the world. A city set on a hill cannot be hidden; nor does anyone light a lamp and put it under a basket, but on the lampstand, and it gives light to all who are in the house. Let your light shine before men in such a way that they may see your good works, and glorify your Father who is in heaven" (Matthew 5:13-16). Equating believers with salt of the earth, Jesus advises that although we are chosen to spread the good news of His gospel, "...if the salt has become tasteless, how can it be made salty *again?* It is no longer good for anything, except to be thrown out and trampled under foot by men" (Matthew 5:13). With this same desire to safeguard believers from becoming "tasteless," Paul directs us to do whatever we do to the glory of God (Colossians 3:23).

One way for believers to reflect on this is to consider that if we would be ashamed for Jesus to see what we are doing, hear what we are saying, or know what is our intention, then it is not right and cannot be done for the glory of God. All we do is for His glory! What we do in this world must lead to becoming more and more like Him (Romans 8:29), and this is only possible if we have continuous maturing in our walk.

"Therefore I urge you, brethren, by the mercies of God, to present your bodies a living and holy sacrifice, acceptable to God, which is your spiritual service of worship. And do not be conformed to this world, but be transformed by the renewing of your mind, so that you may prove what the will of God is, that which is good and acceptable and perfect" (Romans 12:1-2). The first step of any believer's journey is to offer their life to Jesus––to willingly announce to Him, "I am in need of a Savior, and from here forward, I live for You and only for You!" A new believer must decide if they will indeed be a living sacrifice. This means to live 100 percent for Jesus; it means doing the things He would do. Believers work toward this by putting others first before themselves, by loving people whether or not they "deserve" it, and by living as an example of Christ's love and forgiveness regardless of the situation or circumstances.

To be a living sacrifice means we cannot be like everyone else or seek acceptance from other people. It means instead of taking the easy road of conforming to the world, believers answer the call of God to live for Jesus. In practice, this means making a commitment to follow Christ in every area of life, to answer Jesus' directive to "...take up [your] cross daily, and follow Me" (Luke 9:23).

While someone might *believe* in Jesus, this does not necessarily mean they are *following* Jesus; even demons *believe* (James 2:19). As Jesus states, to follow Him we must deny ourselves, and we must each take up our own cross and live for Christ alone. This is not a one-time pronouncement, but a daily battle. It is a commitment that must be renewed over and over again.

As believers, we are called to live for Jesus. We are called to take control of our thoughts and actions and to allow God to transform us into something holy. God can transform and make ugliness into beauty.

Arguably, one of the ugliest bugs is the caterpillar. It is nothing more than a fat little worm with feet. Even so, through God's plan, that twelve-eyed bug is wholly transformed into a beautiful and colorful butterfly. God does not want us to remain as we are; He wants to change our lives for His glory. When we not only believe but actually follow Jesus, we are transformed into a beautiful and living sacrifice. We must choose how we will live.

As Peter urges, "Therefore, prepare your minds for action, keep sober *in spirit*, set your hope completely on the grace to be brought to you at the revelation of Jesus Christ. As obedient children, do not be conformed to the former lusts *which were yours* in your ignorance, but like the Holy One who called you, be holy yourselves also in all *your* behavior; (1 Peter 1:13-15). This sounds like hard work, right? It is hard to turn away from being self-seeking, self-centered, and stubborn! But, if we want to grow, we need to do the hard work, and Christ will help. Are you ready to ask Him for His help?

In 2 Corinthians Paul writes, "Therefore if anyone is in Christ, *this person* is a new creation; the old things passed away; behold, new things have come" (5:17). This book is designed to help believers grow in Christ by shedding the old and living as a new creation. As a living sacrifice, are you ready to stop crawling off the altar of the Lord? Are you prepared to focus your mind, life, and action on a meaningful relationship with Jesus? If yes, then read on! The journey is just beginning, so keep seeking as we delve deeply into Romans 12:1-2 to better understand what it means to give our body, mind, and will over to transformation in Christ!

Chapter Two

A LOADED WORD

**Therefore I urge you, brethren by the
mercies of God,... (Romans 12:1)**

People have a way of tugging at our heartstrings, or at least our obligation-strings. Often we can hear it coming with loaded words like, "if it's not too much trouble," "if you wouldn't mind," or some other phrase that is loaded with emotion and obligation. It is not uncommon for a mom to begin this type of request to her grown child by recalling the story of her heartburn-laden pregnancy and the eleven hour labor that led to the birth of a newborn weighing more than ten pounds. We have all experienced this ask, and perhaps more importantly, we have all done it ourselves.

Not too long ago, I employed this type of ask with one of the teachers at the school ministry where I work. She is amazingly gifted at decorating the bulletin boards here at the school and church, and I wanted to ask her to once again lend her talents on a project. So, I knocked on the door of her classroom where she teaches Spanish, and I asked, "¿Cuanto me quieres, Señora? Porque yo te quiero mucho!" (Translation: "How much do you love me, ma'am? Because I love you lots!") Of course, she started laughing and asked me what I wanted from her. She knows that I am fully aware that she loves it when I attempt to speak Spanish, and so this strategy works for me a lot of the time. Although it is not always so obvious (or intentional), people play the how *much do you love me* card on each other all the time!

Have you ever been in a long, perhaps inconvenient, conversation that seemed to be (finally) winding up when you suddenly hear, "Before you go, the reason I called is...." Or, perhaps you have been in a meeting with the boss who finished a lengthy to-do list only to add, "just one more thing." These are all loaded words that inherently contain all the reasons why we should follow through with whatever it is that the person is asking.

These loaded words can be stressful or even scary. Whether they come from a parent, sibling, child, friend, neighbor, co-worker, boss, or someone else, it can be intimidating to face these emotion-laden asks that carry with them the intrinsic obligation of love, responsibility, or gratitude. Even so, these loaded words are so familiar that they automatically call us to action.

In the book of Romans, Paul uses "therefore" in this manner, imbuing love, responsibility, and gratitude in his call to action. In fact, he uses it eight times to call believers to act on what he has written. In the original language of the New Testament, *oun* (οὖν) or "therefore" is a means of connecting the dots between the discourse and the resulting action. Paul used it to mean that having heard all this, here is what you should do. It's a way of tying the two parts together. I said I was hungry; therefore, I should seek food. This example is an oversimplification, of course, because Paul is not calling us to something as simplistic as a meal. He's indicating that the actions he exhorts us to are natural responses to the truth he has laid out in the text.

In Romans 12:1 for example, Paul uses the word "therefore" as an incitement to action. He is not basing this on his own apostolic authority or on his role as a church planter, nor is he manipulating believers from the position of a spiritual mentor. He is simply calling on us to change, to shape up, to get on track, based on the first eleven chapters of this letter to the Romans, based on the knowledge we already have of Christ and our understanding of God.

In other words, the call to action comes from what Paul had already laid out in Romans:

- The good news of Christ is able to save, change, and convict people (1:16-18).
- God uses nature to reveal His existence (1:19-20).
- Condemnation awaits those rejecting God (2).
- We and all of the world are covered in sin and deserving of condemnation (3:9-20).
- Jesus justifies us (3:24) as a payment for sin (3:25).

This is eternity changing! Ponder for a moment Paul's words: "Therefore I urge you, brethren, *by the mercies of God,*" (12:1a, emphasis added). Through our faith, salvation is awarded. Sin makes us unrighteous, but because He applies His righteousness to us, we no longer have to choose sin (12:4-6). "Therefore there is now no condemnation for those who are in Christ Jesus" (8:1). Consider, too, Israel's pattern of rejection and repentance that was answered by God's love and patience demonstrated to them again and again (chs. 9-11). Because there is no condemnation (8:1), we can never be separated from God's love even through sin, guilt, demons, the world, the flesh, or even death (8:26-39).

Just as we use loaded words to impart the love, responsibility, and/or gratitude that precedes our ask, Paul uses "therefore" to carry the weight and significance of all that is ours in faith. *This* is why Paul's exhortation should spur us to action. His ask is beyond Mom's pressure, more charming than my attempts to speak Spanish, stronger than Grandma's guilt trip, and greater than Paul. It is God, and it is all He is, does, and has planned. As if God Himself is saying, because of Me, because of Who I am and what I have done, I want to see this transformation in your life.

Paul enhances the loaded word "therefore" by adding "I urge you." The Greek word *parakaleō* (παρακαλέω), meaning "to beseech, to beg, to plead, to encourage," stems from *para* meaning "beside" and *kaléō* "to call." It was used in legal proceedings when the court called a witness to give account of something. Paul is asking for an account (a witness) to be given for all Jesus has done for us.

Paul's word selection furthers the emotional component of his plea for believers to act in accordance with what we know of Christ. On behalf of the Savior and His mercies, Paul is begging us to take a moment to think and then to respond in action. Paul lays out all that God has done for us and then asks for a response.

Our response is based on what we think about God's kindness, grace, love, and mercy. It is based on how we view Paul's testimony delivered in chapters 1 through 11 of Romans. In fact, Paul says, "by the mercies of God" (12:1), and let us not forget that by definition receiving mercy is *not* getting what we actually deserve.

It may be true that left to our own devices many of us would feel we deserve greatness and grandeur, but in light of Romans chapters 1 through eleven, we are left pondering David's statement in Psalm 8:4, "What is man that You take thought of him, And the son of man that You care for him ?" We have to ask God, why do you care so much for me when I have done so little for You, and when I could never merit your love, kindness, grace, mercy, or affection?

It is His mercy. This is the 700 pound gorilla in the room that cannot be ignored. God freely gives to us what we do not deserve. His mercy makes each of us family and an heir to His throne. Paul subtly reminds us of even this, calling us brethren. There is so much we deserve but we do not receive (mercy) and so much we do not deserve but we receive anyway (grace), and it is all only because of Jesus. Mercy saves.

> Mademoiselle Lajolais once approached Napoleon seeking a pardon for her father. The emperor replied that the man had committed the same crime against the state twice, and justice demanded death. "But I don't ask for justice," the daughter explained, "I plead for mercy." "But your father does not deserve anything," Napoleon replied. "Sir," the woman cried, "it would not be mercy if he deserved it, and mercy is all that I ask for." "Well then," the emperor said, "I will have mercy." And he spared the woman's son.[1]

---

[1] The Napolean Series, "Research Subjects: Napolean Himself," http://www.napoleon-

God's mercy is ours. He has divinely spared us by His grace. He has showered us with such deep and abiding love that He put His Son on the cross. He continually demonstrates His mercy as He does not give us the punishment, segregation, and consequences that our sin deserves. Brothers and sisters, because Jesus has done so much for us, this is why Paul is asking that we give something back and why he uses the loaded words of "therefore" and "I urge you."

But, Paul does not leave us confused about what we are to do. He does not leave it up to us to choose our offering. He does not leave open to interpretation how we are to respond. He provides us direction on how to give back to God for being such an awesome God, and I know why he does. Because, left to our devices, we choose ourselves.

I remember in the early 1990's my fifteen-year-old brother saved his money from bagging groceries at Winn-Dixie to buy the entire family Christmas presents. This was such a sweet gesture for him to do. I remember going with him to the mall to pick out some presents. But along the way going from store to store, getting our mom a beaded belt and each of our four sisters something from Bath and Body Works, he must have realized he was running out of money, because when it came to getting my dad a gift, he didn't get him the Levi jean shorts my dad had worn every day since either of us were born. No, he turned into Pacific Sunwear, a Generation X teenage surf and skate shop. He bought "my dad" the biggest and baggiest pair of jean shorts he could find. On Christmas day, when my dad

---

series.org/research/napoleon/PopularHistory/Book4/c_popularbook4chapter1.html.

opened the gift, my brother said, "well if you don't like it, I can always keep them and get you something else."

I choose me; it is not uncommon. Most of us, left to our own choices, will choose what hurts me the least, what is the least effort for me, what is least risky for me, what makes me feel good, and so on. Recognizing this and knowing the true nature of man's selfishness, Paul gives us just one option; he points us in only one direction.

Chapter Three

A MOMENT BEFORE THE KING

...to present your bodies... (Romans 12:1)

"If I knew you were coming over, I would have brushed my teeth and showered this week!" My dad's famous for these words when people come to visit. But in actuality, my dad is obsessive when it comes to personal cleanliness. Growing up, when my dad came home from work he was concerned that his work clothes would transfer dirt to us, so he would kiss us on the head and head to the shower. It was only after that shower that we could hug him. In his presence, you had better have clean, trimmed nails, swabbed ears, and be smelling like Irish Spring, or you would be hearing from Dad.

My mom has a similar obsession with keeping a clean home. For her, the house is not clean unless you can smell the bleach. She moves furniture around, dusting, scrubbing and polishing everything. My mom and dad having obsessions with cleanliness is both ironic and challenging with twenty-two grandchildren and three great-grandchildren. There are plenty of stories of cleanliness gone awry.

When I was nine, my parents' first grandchild and my much-loved niece, Ariel, was born to my eldest sister Yvette. In those days, every Friday was spaghetti night at our house, and my sister and her husband joined us almost every Friday. One particular Friday my parents were to host a home Bible study for the church, so the house was extra clean.

I remember Ariel being enthralled with our plates of spaghetti as she sat eating mushy baby food. Eventually, Yvette prepared a small bowl of pasta for Ariel, and she was overjoyed! She loved it so much she decided to wear it, to play with it, to throw it, and to smear it all over herself and everything within her reach. Within minutes she was covered in sauce, noodles and parmesan and so was everything around her.

This might have been less shocking if my parents were not just a few hours from the home Bible study and the arrival of all their guests. My mom and dad sprang into action as the rest of us ooh-ed and aah-ed over the cuteness of Ariel's first spaghetti dinner. My dad ran to the bathtub carrying Ariel outstretched in front of him as far as his arms would reach. Meanwhile, my mom grabbed her cleaning supplies, and sure enough, within minutes, it was as if the entire scene had never happened.

Later, my mom and dad admitted the depth of their panic. However, on that night as we sat reading from Through the Bible with J. Vernon McGee and singing flock songs, no one would have ever imagined the carnage my niece had inflicted with a bowl of spaghetti or the panic she induced in her grandparents. What the people in attendance that evening saw was that the house was presentable, clean, and tidy with everything (and everyone) in place.

That is what presentation is all about: looking your best, having things neat and orderly. This type of presentation, a best first look, is the key to good marketing, business success, and even Hollywood box office hits. After all, it is the movie or television show trailer that gets our attention. It's the attraction that catches our eye, and the reason we come back for more.

In Romans 12:1 Paul has us thinking along these same lines. Is there a moment in your life that you can remember saying, "Jesus, my life is for you?" This is what Paul is saying; have that moment, give your self over to Jesus because of what He has done for you, for each of us. If we are to present our bodies, we are about to have a significant moment, so we should want to give our very best.

The Greek word used here is *parastésai*. It was used in the Old Testament when an animal was being presented for sacrifice, or when a priest was presenting an offering on the altar. This word comes from two separate words, *para,* meaning "from" or "in the presence of," and *histémi,* meaning "to stand" or "to place oneself." Together the meaning is "to exhibit yourself." It is a literal presentation, but not of a thing or an idea. Instead, it is a presentation of your own self as an act of worship.

A presentation is a defining moment at a specific time, where a display takes place. For believers, this consequential offering of self in an eternity-changing moment is the surrender to Jesus, the acknowledgement of our need for a Savior. Each of us as believers has that moment in our life when we say, "Jesus, my life is for You" and where we present our own self to Christ our Savior.

This is what Paul is talking about, about that moment when for all He has done for us we give ourselves to Jesus, and not just *to* Jesus, but *back to* Jesus. It is the moment a believer can point to and say this is when I laid my life at the feet of the King, no gold or silver would do, but instead I presented my being, my self, the only thing I could offer, my life for Christ to use.

This is the moment Paul is asking us to enter into with our Savior; a moment of presenting ourselves to the King. In movies, books, and even news media, when people come before a king, they do not arrive empty-handed. I always thought it strange that people would visit royalty and bring some type of gift as if to say, "I know you are rich and powerful, so here is a bunch of monkeys, some wild game, and a few jewels." Why is that? It seems likely that a king would already have these types of things.

Perhaps it is because when we stand before royalty, when we are in the presence of greatness, when we have the honor of being in the presence of one who is awe-inspiring, we are compelled to offer what we have to give. When we are before the King of Kings, we are saying, "What I have is yours, and to prove my loyalty, I offer all I have to give to you."

In other words, our presentation before the Lord is a pledge; it is saying, what we have is His, what we have is devoted to Him, and who we are is aligned with the Lord. Have you had that moment yet? That moment when you say, "Okay, Lord, here I am!" Even the wise men knew that to honor a king in his presence is to come bearing gifts, and they did. When they stood before Jesus, they offered gold, frankincense, and myrrh. But what do we have to offer to the King?

Gifts of gold and silver are well and good, but we know that these metals are flooring material in heaven; the streets are paved with gold (Revelation 21:21). Giving Jesus gifts of gold and silver would be like standing before the queen of England holding a bag of asphalt! Standing in the presence of our Savior, we want to give something of value.

Consider why Jesus came to the earth in the first place. It was to die on a cross so we would not be separated from Him for all eternity, and instead that we would be reunited with Him. It was to restore the relationship between God and man that was stained by sin. It was to bring us back into communion with God.

> For if the blood of goats and bulls and the ashes of a heifer sprinkling those who have been defiled sanctify for the cleansing of the flesh, how much more will the blood of Christ, who through the eternal Spirit offered Himself without blemish to God, cleanse your conscience from dead works to serve the living God? For this reason He is the mediator of a new covenant, so that, since a death has taken place for the redemption of the transgressions that were *committed* under the first covenant, those who have been called may receive the promise of the eternal inheritance. For where a covenant is, there must of necessity be the death of the one who made it (Hebrews 9:13-16).

Jesus cares so much for us that He was willing to pay the high price for our redemption. The payment was more precious than any other; Christ died for us. He died for you, and He died for me. Take this to heart: the King of Kings died for us because in His view we are the most valuable of all things. He died for us because we are worth the price to Him. So, when we stand before our Savior, when we are in His presence, we must be prepared to give ourselves, the only gift of any worth.

Through His covenant of grace, we are purchased from sin with the body of Jesus Christ. "But He was pierced for our offenses, He was crushed for our wrongdoings; The punishment for our well-being *was laid* upon Him, And by His wounds we are healed" (Isaiah 53:5). As believers, this is the moment of our freedom, the moment we become undeserving recipients of God's grace, mercy and love. Jesus presented Himself to the Father as payment for our sin, as the mark of the new covenant, the covenant sealed by His blood. Because of this, you and I have the opportunity to offer Him ourselves, living for Him in truth and loving others in action.

You may be thinking: Seriously? Does God really want *me*? The answer is: Yes! Absolutely! The fact is that God wants you entirely. The Greek word *sóma* (σῶμα) means "body." It comes from the root *sós* (σῶς), meaning "entire."[2] He wants all of you, and me, and every one of us, and we are called to give ourselves back to Him with everything in us.

Mark 12:28-30, known to Jews as the Shema, presents to us Jesus' own directives for our relationship with him: "One of the scribes came up and heard them arguing, and recognizing that He had answered them well, asked Him, 'What commandment is the foremost of all?' Jesus answered, 'The foremost is, "HEAR, ISRAEL! THE LORD IS OUR GOD, THE LORD IS ONE; AND YOU SHALL LOVE THE LORD YOUR GOD WITH ALL YOUR HEART, AND WITH ALL YOUR SOUL, AND WITH ALL YOUR MIND, AND WITH ALL YOUR STRENGTH."''" This explanation by Jesus forms the essential directive for each of us in our personal relationship with Him; we are to love Him with heart, mind, and soul, exhausting every ounce of strength.

When we love the Lord with all our might, the second directive we are given to grow in our relationship with Jesus, to

---

[2] Joseph Thayer, *Thayer's Greek-English Lexicon of the New Testament* (Peabody, MA: Hendrickson, 2007), 611.

love our neighbor as ourselves (Mark 12:31), seems a natural progression. But, what does it mean to love the Lord with heart, soul, mind, and strength? Perhaps the specific words spoken in the scripture can further inform us.

- **Heart**, original Greek is *kardias* (καρδίας), the center and vigor of physical life.[3]
- **Soul**, original Greek is *psyches* (ψυχῆς), breath, life sustainer.[4]
- **Mind**, original Greek is *dianoias* (διανοίας), thoughts and understanding.[5]
- **Strength**, original Greek is *ischyos* (ἰσχύος), ability, force, and might.[6]

Considering these meanings, it becomes clear that we are called to let our love for the Lord overtake all that we are. Jesus is saying that this is the most important thing to do. He is saying that our love for Him should consume our being (heart), essence (soul), and thoughts (mind), and not only this, but to do so with every bit of ability and might we have, reserving or withholding nothing (strength).

In other words, the love we have for the Lord needs to be an all-consuming love. This is the kind of presentation of ourselves that Jesus is asking from us. He is asking for this love we have for Him to overtake us to the point where it consumes every aspect of us and causes us to say, "Here I am Lord. I am

---

[3] Joseph Thayer. *Thayer's Greek-English Lexicon of the New Testament* (Peabody, MA: Hendrickson, 2007), 325.
[4] Thayer, 677.
[5] Thayer, 140.
[6] Thayer, 307-308.

presenting myself a living sacrifice consumed by your grace, mercy, and love. I am overwhelmed and have nothing to offer You except myself. My love for you, God, has taken over every area of my life, my actions, and thoughts, my very being. Lord, I am so in love with you, and because of all you have done I am offering myself, I am presenting all of me, my thoughts, my life, my actions, my power, my strength, all I am offered to the Great I Am."

To love God is to offer your body, and to allow Him to have control in your life. This may feel contradictory, but upon greater review, it makes sense that these two would be halves of the whole. They form the answer to the question: In my daily life, what does it look like to do as Jesus directs?

Chapter Four

¡SÍ! ¿CÓMO NO?

...a living and holy sacrifice, acceptable to God... (Romans 12:1)

I grew up in Miami, and I love Miami for its culture and the eccentric way of life people embrace here. It really is unique unto itself. Although an oversimplification, you could say that Miami is where Caribbean meets South America meets capitalism, and arguably, it only makes sense in the context of Miami. Perhaps a suitable catchphrase for Miami might be, "¡Sí! ¿Cómo no?" The translation is "Sure, why not?" Of course, as is the case with many translations, this one does not convey the full meaning intended by the one using it.

¡Sí! ¿Cómo no? is a phrase that is generally quite casual, "Sure, why not?" However, if it is expressed emphatically enough, it conveys a sense of excitement or even an "all in" thrill. It is this excited response expressing "Yes! I'm in!" which best reflects Miami.

Consider the weather here in Miami. December may mean winter in other places, but in Miami we ask if anyone wants to go to the beach, and what is Miami's response? ¡Sí! ¿Cómo no? Yes! I'm in! The same is true for the night life. While the rest of Florida and much of the nation is heading to bed at night, Miami is asking if anyone wants to go out and have some fun, ¡Sí! ¿Cómo no? Yes! I'm in!

In Romans, Paul is calling believers with the same excited invitation. In response to all that Jesus has done for us, Paul is inviting us to lay ourselves down as a living sacrifice, to say, "Yes! I'm in!" Like heading to the beach when it is supposed to be winter, or leaving the house to start the evening when everyone else is heading to sleep, dying to self in order to live may seem counterintuitive. However, for Christians, dying to self in order to live makes perfect sense, and as believers our enthusiastic response is—Yes! I'm in! We are excited to give it all to Jesus for all He has done, because nothing in this world makes more sense than that. It may seem counterintuitive in thought, but it makes complete actionable sense for believers.

Now, how do we go about laying ourselves down as a living sacrifice? Paul is not calling us to literally sacrifice ourselves physically on an altar before God. Instead, he is calling us to put everything we are and everything we have into subjection to God and to no longer live for ourselves and our own selfish desires. This goes hand in hand with loving God with all that we are, our very being, and to living for Him with all we have, think, and do.

As a living sacrifice, we are no longer free to act on fleshly impulse or selfish desires. Instead, our wants and needs have become secondary to Jesus—Yes! I'm in! ¡Sí! ¿Cómo no? Luke records Jesus' own words on following Him, which are the foundation of Paul's invitation: "And He was saying to them *all*, 'If anyone wants to come after Me, he must deny himself, take up his cross daily, and follow Me'" (Luke 9:23).

How much do you love Jesus? Are you ready to stop crawling off the altar? Do you love Him with all of who and what you are, with your whole being? Do you love Him enough to reject yourself?—enough to stop doing what comes naturally? Are you willing to stop living in sin?—willing to risk being rejected by the world? Are you committed to attending to the needs of others above and before your own? Are you prepared to speak up for Christ when deep inside you feel like it is easier or safer to keep silent? Are you ready to die so you can live?

Dying to our selfish thinking and pride, and to our natural desires to pursue worldly success and chase pleasures of the flesh actually sets us free, free to live like Jesus, to live as a light for Him, pleasing Him, and glorifying Him with our very existence. This freedom is a choice. We cannot live for Him when we are shackled by worldliness or selfish thinking; we must indeed die with the old things having passed away so that we can live as a new creation in Jesus (see 2 Corinthians 5:17).

It could be said that following Jesus costs believers their lives. It is a decision that is lived out as a commitment. Jesus tells us that it is a commitment we must make again each and every day. It is waking in the morning saying, "Lord, this day is for You, my life is for You, my words are for You, my finances are for You. Help me be You for others today, and to love You the way You deserve to be loved!" When we do this, when we make the decision to stop crawling off the altar, an amazing thing happens; God's love that we are drawn into makes us holy.

When Paul calls us to be a living, holy sacrifice, he does so intending for us to understand what holy means. The Greek term *hágios* (ἅγιος) means "something set apart by or for God." It is a special designation identifying that we no longer live for self. We no longer live in selfishness, self-interest, self-preservation, and self-centered thinking. When we present ourselves a living sacrifice subjected to our King, we are set apart for holy use.

If the president of the United States was coming to dinner, we would not serve him corndogs and tater tots on paper plates or tap water in a red Solo® cup. In presenting the meal to someone of this renown, we would serve beef bourginon on fine china and Perrier® in crystal glasses. The meal would be a special event for an even more special individual. The presentation and preparation would be far from ordinary, and our goal would be perfection, or at least as close as we could get to it.

This is exactly the point that Paul is making about the presentation of our own self before Jesus. Our set-apart self is special not because of who we are or what we do, but because of who we are presenting ourselves to (Christ), and because of why we are presenting ourselves to Him (to glorify Him). Our presentation is valuable because of the purpose He has for us and how that purpose glorifies Him.

Do not misunderstand. This is not easy. It takes someone special to make this commitment to live for the Lord and to serve only Him. Furthermore, it takes an enormous amount of love to act on this commitment day after day after day, but we are not alone. God is not calling us to anything He Himself has not already done, nor is He calling us to anything we are not able to do.

Paul writes, "I have been crucified with Christ; and it is no longer I who live, but Christ lives in me; and the *life* which I now live in the flesh I live by faith in the Son of God, who loved me and gave Himself up for me" (Galatians 2:20). Paul's words, "I have been crucified" mean that he is already dead to the power of sin and this world. He is saying that, essentially, we are all dead men walking, dead to the things of this world, and alive forever in Christ. Personally, I have had my moment of presenting myself before my Savior as a living sacrifice, I left everything there before Him, and now I am living my life in praise of Him. My life is His, and I daily confirm my commitment to follow Him. The decision is yours. Are you prepared to leave your self at the altar? Are you ready to say, "Yes! I'm in! ¡Sí! ¿Cómo no?"

Unless we are distinguishing ourselves as saved by Christ, in the world but no longer of the world, we might as well be serving Him corndogs and tater tots on paper plates and tap water in a red Solo® cup. Simply put, the old self needs to go; it must die! Christ is worthy of all we have, of our very best. It is time we prepare the beef bourginon, bring down the fine china, and polish the crystal.

Not long ago in Miami, we had a freeze for three or four days. The timing was unfortunate; I had just planted two Haiden Mango trees, one in my front yard and one in the back. As protection from the freezing cold, I wrapped my outdoor plants. More accurately, I wrapped almost all of my outdoor plants. There were five that I did not get to that first night, including the two new mango trees. Before the second night, I wrapped the remaining five. Once the freeze had passed, I uncovered my plants. Over the next few days, I watched helplessly as the five plants that had been exposed that first night slowly turned brown.

Dismayed, I recalled that it was important to remove dead or dying parts from the plants so they did not draw on the limited resources the plants had to sustain life. So, I spent time carefully removing all the leaves and any dead sticks and branches from the plants in the backyard. Later, on the advice of my mother, I bought some spray fertilizer and fed the backyard plants weekly.

My efforts paid off and all of the plants in the backyard were rejuvenated. The only plant that did not survive was the mango tree in the front yard. I realized that I had not taken the time to remove all the dead or dying leaves from the tree in the front yard, and I had not been routinely fertilizing it as I had done for the plants in the backyard. I did not put the care and feeding into the front yard mango tree, and it failed to thrive.

In the same way, if we are going to grow in Christ, the old must go and our growth must be fed. In other words, if we leave the dead bits they will just leach the nutrition away and our growth will be stunted or absent altogether. Growth has two parts, trim away the dead and dying (old self), and also feed the growth with high-quality nutrition (the word of God).

The old self is our innate human nature, our natural desires toward self-indulgence and self-preservation. Paul directs us to lay the old self aside writing, "Do not lie to one another, since you stripped off the old self with its *evil* practices, and have put on the new *self,* which is being renewed to a true knowledge according to the image of the One who created it—" (Colossians 3:9-10). The original Greek lays out this directive in no uncertain terms, using *apekduomai* (ἀπεκδύομαι) meaning "laid, disarm, to strip off"[7] and *palaios* (παλαιός) meaning "old, worn out by use" as in how one was before change.[8]

When we become new, our new self is God-seeking, which is diametrically opposed to the natural state of man. We 34ophia live our new life in Jesus Christ with our old, worldly, dying self

---

[7] Thayer and Smith, "Apekduomai" in *The NAS New Testament Greek Lexicon,* electronic.
[8] Thayer and Smith, "Palaios".

still holding on. If we do, there cannot be new, life-sustaining growth; the old will starve out the new, and it will not thrive. Are you holding onto the dead leaves of your old self and keeping your new self in Jesus from growing? Are you offering the Lord what is left over rather than offering all of you?

Leaving behind a life that is self-focused and self-centered to embrace one that is Christ centered and others focused represents an enormous shift, but it is living this life in the new self that makes us acceptable and pleasing to God. To make such an immense change is monumental, and so it is clear why Paul supports his plea with the enormity of all Jesus has done for us.

Of course, most of us do not give sufficient thought to what it means to be pleasing to God. We are usually so focused on the minutia of our own desires and the pursuit of our own pleasure that we do not think about what makes God happy. Yet, if we are offering ourselves as a sacrifice to Him, should we not do it for His pleasure?

Consider the animal sacrifices performed in the Old Testament. They were made in response to God's anger about the Israelites' sin which resulted in God distancing Himself from them. The purpose of the sacrifices was to please God, to draw Him near, and to bring His favor back upon His people.

In the Old Testament there are many references to sacrifice having a pleasing aroma to the Lord. Leviticus alone has a number of references including 1:9, 2:2, 3:5, 4:31, 6:15, 8:21, 23:13. The pleasing aroma was not about the odor of an animal or grain offering, but about the fact that God was pleased by the Israelites' desire to atone for their sin and seek redemption.

The same atonement for sin and accomplishment of redemption is reflected in Christ's death on the cross. As believers, we have once and for all redemption because of Christ. Even so, in the New Testament we are called to be living sacrifices that please God. Paul points this out, writing about believers: "For we are a fragrance of Christ to God" (2 Corinthians 2:15a). Humility is beautiful in God's sight. Seeking forgiveness and choosing not to sin again is a beautiful thing; it pleases God like a fragrant aroma. Would you describe your life as a fragrant aroma to God?

In Luke 7:36-50, the story of Jesus' compassion for a repentant sinner is related.

> "Now one of the Pharisees invited Jesus to have dinner with him, so he went to the Pharisee's house and reclined at the table. When a woman who had lived a sinful life in that town learned that Jesus was eating at the Pharisee's house, she brought an alabaster jar of perfume, and as she stood behind him at his feet weeping, she began to wet his feet with her tears. Then she wiped them with her hair, kissed them and poured perfume on them. When the Pharisee who had invited him saw this, he said to himself, "If this man were a prophet, he would know who is touching him and what kind of woman she is—that she is a sinner." Jesus answered him, "Simon, I have something to tell you." "Tell me, teacher," he said. "Two men owed money to a certain moneylender. One owed him five hundred denarii, and the other fifty. Neither of them had the money to pay him back, so he canceled the debts of both. Now which of them will love him more?" Simon replied, "I suppose the one who had the bigger debt canceled." "You have judged correctly," Jesus said. Then he turned toward the woman and said to Simon, "Do you

see this woman? I came into your house. You did not give me any water for my feet, but she wet my feet with her tears and wiped them with her hair. You did not give me a kiss, but this woman, from the time I entered, has not stopped kissing my feet. You did not put oil on my head, but she has poured perfume on my feet. Therefore, I tell you, her many sins have been forgiven–for she loved much. But he who has been forgiven little loves little." Then Jesus said to her, "Your sins are forgiven." The other guests began to say among themselves, "Who is this who even forgives sins?" Jesus said to the woman, "Your faith has saved you; go in peace" (Luke 7:36-50).

The woman, apparently a prostitute, came to Jesus in search of forgiveness. She poured out all she had as an offering, including her desire to be forgiven, her tears, and a bottle of expensive perfume which she poured out onto Jesus' feet (vv. 36-38). When her presence as a street person and her action in wasting expensive perfume was called out, Jesus explained that it was precisely because of the enormity of her sin that He was moved by the pouring out of her sorrow, grief, and pain. He identified that the greater the debt, the more grateful the debtor who is forgiven it (vv. 39-43). He further identified that the depth of her faith in our loving and merciful God, brought her before Jesus offering her sacrifice of all she had (vv. 44-50). In response, His forgiveness is poured out, and He assures her "Your faith has saved you; go in peace" (Luke 7:50).

This woman did not have much; she did not even possess a reputation of any worth. However, withholding nothing, what little she did have she brought to the feet of Jesus. She understood her place, and like the widow who gave everything available for her survival (Luke 21:1-4), she withheld absolutely nothing. She took whatever was at her disposal as a means of coming before Jesus, even if it was only her hair. "Does not even nature itself teach you that if a man has long hair, it is a dishonor to him, but if a woman has long hair, it is a glory to her? For her hair is given to her for a covering" (1 Corinthians 11:14-15).

She took the glory she did have and used it to wipe the feet of Jesus. She showered Him with tears, kisses, and expensive perfume, and used her covering to wipe His feet, the same feet that carried the news of salvation. Shortly after this encounter, Jesus' feet would walk the road to Golgotha and be nailed to the cross for the sins of the world. Even His feet are worthy of honor. Everything the woman did illustrated her own humility as it demonstrated her desire to honor to Jesus. In this scripture, Jesus points out that this is in contrast with even those closest to Him, calling out Simon for having done nothing similar for Jesus (Luke 7:44-46).

Like many of us today, Simon was in need of a reality check. He did not honor Christ by treating him as a special guest; in fact, Jesus points out that Simon treated Him as any common guest. This was evidenced by the fact that Simon did not treat Jesus as an honored guest according to the custom of the time. If Simon had treated Jesus as an honored guest, more important than himself, he would have greeted Jesus with a double kiss, he would have anointed His head with olive oil, and he would have had a servant wash Jesus' feet. But Simon had done none of these things; he did not see himself as less important or lower than Christ. Simon had behaved as any of us would when entertaining a friend.

It is not uncommon for us to forget our place in relationship to greatness. A college girl visiting the museum at Beethoven's home, slipped under the rope and began playing Beethoven's piano. When approached by personnel, she said offhandedly, "I suppose every musician who comes here wants to play this piano." The man responded by sharing with her that during a recent visit by the great Paderewski an invitation to sit at the piano and play was extended to him. Paderewski replied, "No, I do not feel worthy to play the great master's piano."[9]

Simon's offering was one between equals. He invited Jesus to join him and to share a meal together as friends. This is not what Jesus wants from us. When we offer ourselves it must be in humility and a recognition of our lowliness, fully understanding that it is His unparalleled sacrifice that purchased our salvation.

Are you like Simon? Are you laying down all you have at the feet of Jesus, seeing your greatest possession as His? Or, are you simply entertaining a friend? If we are not giving our all in humility, if we are not subjecting ourselves and our lives to Him, we are just entertaining a treasured friend. But, we know this is not the case. Even as we give all we have, our offering of a life of love lived for Him, it pales in comparison to His great sacrifice on the cross, and all we can do is lay down our offering of honor, humility, and a life lived in love for His glory.

The offering that pleases God has a sweet aroma of love, humility, forgiveness, and self-sacrifice. Our offerings, done in this way, please the Lord so much because they are moments lived out that cannot be repossessed or taken back. Like the woman of ill repute who poured out the expensive perfume, once

---

[9] James Hewett, *Illustrations Unlimited* (Carol Stream, IL: Tyndale, 1988), 294.

the jar was broken, the scented oil was never going to be recaptured, the value of it was given, and the offering was total and complete. This is the same finality of the once and for all sacrifice of Jesus on the cross; "and walk in love, just as Christ also loved you and gave Himself up for us, an offering and a sacrifice to God as a fragrant aroma" (Ephesians 5:2).

Jesus' sacrifice on the cross was unto death; it was total and complete. He did not stop after the beatings at the hands of the temple guards, nor did He stop at the scourging. He gave all; there was nothing more to give and no way to take it back. The lesson for us is that our offering of ourselves as living sacrifices is a reflection of the completeness of what He has done for us, and this is what pleases God.

Chapter Five

WORSHIP

...*which* is your spiritual service of worship. (Romans 12:1)

We have all had that experience, driving in the car singing along to our favorite worship song and feeling a deep connection when the song ends and the next one is a completely different style that draws us out of our reverie. In an effort to recapture the moment, we change the radio station or click a different playlist, all because the music did not meet our preferences for worship.

When you hear the word "worship" what comes to mind? If you are like me and millions of others, your thoughts take you to singing praises on Sunday, or to a midweek Bible study where worship is simply a guitar and and a group of people singing along. Or, perhaps you find yourself thinking of a more contemporary worship experience that includes fog coming from a machine in the corner and the flashing of neon lights as the worship leader works a synthesizer. I have to admit, that is definitely not what I think of, but your mind may have gone there.

Whatever we each think of as worship and the opportunity to praise the Lord, no matter how fervent or grandiose, it is nothing more than a drop in the bucket of true worship; it is only faintly scratching the surface of praising the Lord. Worship is the soul crying out for what only Christ can give. It is a cry for belonging and acceptance that only Jesus can provide. It is a longing to fill the God-shaped void in the heart of every human being.

Sometimes we lose sight of why we worship, of who our sung praises are directed toward, of what is the point of a sermon, and even of why we meet together in fellowship in the first place. It's Jesus. It's Jesus, who saved the world through His death and resurrection. Worship is a humbling of ourselves in selfless adoration. The focus of worship is always Jesus; it is never about you, or me, or anyone else as an individual. When we come to it selflessly to glorify Jesus and to praise the Lord for who He is and all that He has done, our act of selflessness actually benefits us. We benefit because the act of worship prepares us for Him, it readies us to work and to focus on Him. The Apostle James tells us, "Humble yourselves before the Lord, and he will lift you up" (James 4:10).

When we approach Jesus in humble adoration, we are accomplishing one part of worship, which is reverence. The original Greek word *eusebés* (εὐσεβής) is used to describe holding one in reverence, in this case, being in awe of the Mighty God. In other words, worship is realizing our place in relationship to our awesome Creator. The prophet Isaiah describes being overcome with amazement as the wonder of God seen (Isaiah 6).

It is this sense of reverence at the awesome wonder of the Savior that compels us. We cannot help but sing out in worship; that is, unless we find ourselves misunderstanding our place in relationship to our Creator. If we lose sight of God and start to hold ourselves in high esteem, it is essential to be reminded of who we once were, where and how we once lived, and what Christ has done for us.

In some ways, worship can be thought of as a thermometer for the soul; the more we know about God the more fevered we become in our unabashed desire to worship Him in every sense. True worship is coming to the spring of life without restraint, shamelessly exposing our souls to the Son. True worship calls for us to expose ourselves in this uninhibited manner in our prayer life, and in our approach to His word as we read it, study it, and hear it. True worship calls for raw and unencumbered exposure as we sing His praise from our lips.

While reverence is one part of worship, praise is another. Praise is the type most commonly associated with the concept of worship. Praise (*aineō*) is what we usually tie to worship and define it as. This singing and the shouts of acclamation that often accompany it are not the source of our worship, but instead represent the outward manifestations of worship. Worship itself, as defined by the specific use of *aineō*, is an overflowing of the awe man feels for the Lord.

> Then I looked, and I heard the voices of many angels around the throne and the living creatures and the elders; and the number of them was myriads of myriads, and thousands of thousands, saying with a loud voice, "Worthy is the Lamb that was slaughtered to receive power, wealth, wisdom, might, honor, glory, and blessing." And I heard every created thing which is in heaven, or on the earth, or under the earth, or on the sea, and all the things in them, saying, "To Him who sits on the throne and to the Lamb *be* the blessing, the honor, the glory, and the dominion forever and ever." And the four living

creatures were saying, "Amen." And the elders fell down and worshiped (Revelation 5:11-14).

True worship is reflected in these passages, where John paints a moving picture of the prayers, singing of praises, and wonder of being filled with truth that he was priviledged to see. This filling up and the overflowing that comes from wonder and awe illustrates yet another type of worship. From the Greek *proskuneó* (προσκυνέω), this worship is literally being overwhelmed and falling down in adoration; it is the act of prostrating oneself before greatness.

As forms of worship—reverence, thanksgiving, and adoration all penetrate and expose the soul. They cause us to be humble because through them we admit our need for the Savior (reverence), we pour out songs of highest praise to the One, the only One, who can meet our need (thanksgiving), and we bow before Him, recognizing His greatness (adoration).

There is another type of worship most commonly related in the Old Testament where it was originally described using the Greek word *thréskeia* (θρησκεία), meaning "ritual acts of worship." Some people today avoid or even fear this type of worship because of its ritualistic style. In Old Testament times, this worship included sacrifices, incense, and ritualized prayers and songs, and while we do not perform sacrifices today, this type of worship is not reserved for the people who lived in ancient times.

James refers to ritual behaviors when he speaks of the new covenant, writing "If anyone thinks himself to be religious, yet does not bridle his tongue but deceives his *own* heart, this person's religion is worthless. Pure and undefiled religion in the sight of *our* God and Father is this: to visit orphans and widows in their distress, *and* to keep oneself unstained by the world" (James 1:26-27). While it is true that its predictability and routine nature may imply it is somehow lesser worship, this is not the case. The routinized, ritual acts that define *thréskeia* worship are pleasing to God, and this is reason enough to take part.

In this passage from the book of James, we observe three characteristics of worship performed as ritual acts: speech, service, and being set apart. This worship is beyond Sunday meetings, praising God with our voices, and tithing our ten percent. It requires us to make a ritual out of worshipping God with how we speak and communicate (speech), how we care for and do for others (service), and how we live a God-pleasing life in this world, not allowing its influences to sway us, but instead being set apart.

As we continue to live in this manner, our actions become rituals because we no longer have to think about each one of them, they flow automatically from a grateful heart. When it comes to speech, James points out that if anyone says they are religious or worshipful but is lying, gossiping, or otherwise bad mouthing, that person is a fake, he is lying to himself (v. 26). We are not worshipping God or in communion with Jesus if we speak any kind of evil. Making a habit of speaking truth in love and kindness establishes a ritual, which is then performed routinely as an act of worship.

This habit that becomes a ritual act of worship extends beyond our speech to acts of caring for others. James specifically identifies that we are to care for those who cannot care for themselves (v. 26). Caring for those in need, for helpless individuals, and for others who are created in God's image just as we are, is an act of worship. When we do this as a matter of routine, we exhibit *thréskeia* worship.

As James points out, authentic believers demonstrate their faith by guarding their speech and caring for others as they divorce themselves from the world's destructive influences (v. 27). Keeping ourselves from worldliness, including desires of the flesh and other lures of darkness, means that although we are living here in this world, we are not the same as this world; it means that we do not act as those who belong to this world. It can be surmised that James is calling us to form habits in our life that are actions of caring, speech, and detachment from sin. He is calling us to make worship in a behavior.

William Booth, founder of the Salvation Army, has been credited with saying, "If a church was on fire for God, people for miles would come to watch it burn."[10] We are called to be these true worshippers, living "on fire for God," honoring the Lord with our lifestyle and acts of service as we worship God in prayer, song, and speech. The apostle John writes, "But a time is coming, and even now has arrived, when the true worshipers will worship the Father in spirit and truth; for such people the Father seeks to *be* His worshipers. God is spirit, and those who worship Him must worship in spirit and truth" (John 4:23-24). As believers, our "on fire for God" worship has the potential to draw crowds to Christ.

One day, a woman came to her pastor in tears. She told him that in her worship she felt empty and disconnected from God. Her tears continued as she related how she had been to churches of every denomination, tried myriad styles of singing,

---

[10] Rick Ezell, "Sermon: The Power of Worship – Psalm 40, John 12," Lifeway.com, January 27, 2014, http://www.lifeway.com/Article/sermon-power-of-worship-psalm-40-john-12.

prayed for every gift in Scripture, and had even had people lay hands on her, yet her emptiness and feeling of distance remained. She finished by telling the pastor that she simply did not feel satisfied and that she needed God to do more. The pastor nodded sympathetically and gently explained that the key to attaining spiritual victory, abiding peace, and true contentment lies not in trying to get something *from* God but to seek in every way to give all that we can *to* Him.

Our problems with emptiness and disconnection come from misplaced focus and intention. It is not about what we can receive; it is about what we can give. We are called to love God with our entire being, and to worship Him in all we do.

This is the "living and holy sacrifice" Paul is speaking about in Romans 12:1. Worship as a lifestyle encompasses everything about us, including our actions and speech. It is reflected in our choice to follow Jesus, to be led by His Spirit instead of by the ways of the world. It is a worship that defines every aspect of a believer's life. This is not about being a spectacle, walking down the street singing hymns to ourselves or randomly bowing to unseen entities. It is a worshipping of God for His glory that is so all consuming that it has overtaken our natural state of selfishness and sin. It is not so much a desire as it is a passion, a life not only lived *for* Him but *because of* Him.

Jesus Himself explains this concept of life lived as worship saying, "You are the light of the world. A city set on a hill cannot be hidden; nor do *people* light a lamp and put it under a basket, but on the lampstand, and it gives light to all who are in the house. Your light must shine before people in such a way that they may see your good works, and glorify your Father who is in heaven" (Matthew 5:14-16). Are we living our lives as worship, dedicated to living for Jesus, choosing daily to follow and to serve Him? When we choose to let our life be like the worship songs we sing, not about us, not about praising ourselves, but about Jesus, about pleasing God, it is then that our light shines before others for the glory of God.

Levitical offerings were made to atone for sin. They were necessary because man is sinful and full of failure. The need to atone was a stark reminder that man could never accomplish redemption for himself because he is sinful and would fall short over and over again. On his own, man would forever be in need of redemption anew. Because of Jesus, we have the once and for all redemption that has freed us forever.

When we choose to be a "living and holy sacrifice" as described in Romans 12:1, it means loving Him, and living in awe of what He has done in sacrificing Himself for us. It is worshipping Him for what He continues to do as He loves us, nurtures us, and grows us. And, it is praising Him for what He is yet to do according to the word of God. It is living in awe, thankfulness, and love, praising God and giving back to Him in worship.

Worship in the form of being a living sacrifice is not a physical death but a spiritual one. The phrase "spiritual service of worship" *logikēn*, has its root in the Greek term *logos*, meaning "the essence of" or "word," and means "reasonable." The essence of our worship is the spiritual offering of our own selves. It is the humble presentation of ourselves to God. It is not just singing praise on Sundays but living praise on every day. The sacrifice we are presenting to God is our life and our decision to die to self and lay ourselves before Him, which is a reasonable way to praise God because of what He has done for us.

When we lay ourselves down as a living sacrifice, our lives become worship, like a musical note sung to the Lord. Though we deserve punishment for the bad things we do, God gives us grace. While we have no right to it, God offers mercy. This is reason enough to live your life like worship, a time you praise God's name no matter the ups and downs! Live your life like a song of praise, crying out in the good times and bad! Let the praises flow, be bent on knee, and let the actions of your life ever be true worship.

These initial chapters were intended to inspire you, and I pray that you had your own "¡Sí! ¿Cómo no?", "Yes! I'm in!" moment. The second half of this book presents the moment of decision, it tackles the next verse in Romans 12, where Paul lays out just what it takes to become a living sacrifice. It is a moment we all face, when we must make a choice. Will we conform to the world and fit ourselves into its mold, or will we break the mold and live a life of worship that is pleasing to God?

Chapter Six

BE A SALMON

And do not be conformed to this world,... (Romans 12:2)

Recently, I watched a video online that demonstrated how quickly people would assimilate themselves into a situation or context in order to fit in or blend in more easily. The scene was set in a doctor's office, where everyone was an actor participating in the ruse except one actual patient, a woman who was not an actor. The patient was not aware she was participating in a social experiment to observe her responses to a specific situation.

The role of the actors was to stand up together in response to a beeping sound, which occurred every five minutes. Using time lapse, the video showed that the first two times the beeping sounded the group of actors stood in unison while the unwitting patient look around uncomfortably. By the third time the beeping sounded, the patient joined the others in standing, and she continued to stand up in response to the beeping from that point on.

As more patients began to arrive for their appointments, the film crew had one actor leave the waiting room each time a new patient arrived. Still, every five minutes the beeping would sound and it would be time to stand up. Eventually, the room had no actors and only patients who were unaware of the experiment. Even so, each time the beeping occurred, the patients continued to stand and then sit again until the next beeping sounded.

Eventually, the film crew sent in a new actor who sat next to the original patient. When the beeping began, she led everyone in standing together while the actor sat pretending to read a newspaper. When he failed to stand, she became agitated, and leaning over she tapped him explaining that at each beeping he was to stand then sit along with everyone else. When the man asked why they were standing when they heard the beeping, the woman looked confused and sheepishly answered, "That's what we do."

When the beeping began again, the same actor remained seated as the woman watched in annoyance. After just three rounds without anything happening, the woman timidly stayed in her chair, too. Slowly, the patients in the waiting room rejected their new "training" and remained seated. The end result being that not only did conformity win, it won twice!

Oh, the things we will do to avoid discomfort or to win a feeling of belonging! It is tempting to follow suit or go with the flow to avoid ruffling feathers and to fit in. It is often hard to do what is right and it can be highly distressing to risk losing acceptance. Conforming may be easier in the moment, but think of how it tarnishes our worship. How many times have we failed, how much growth have we missed, how many rewards have we forfeited, and how many miracles have we missed out on while we were focused on standing at the beep with everyone else?

In Romans 12:2, Paul exhorts us to stop conforming to the world. When we conform to the world, we are being like gelatin that changes shape to accommodate whatever is the shape of the container it is in. When the gelatin is moved to a different container, it simply reconfigures itself to fit the change in circumstances. Put gelatin into a shape and it becomes that shape; it will become a circle, a square, or a triangle. The content of gelatin is also easily manipulated. Add fruit to the gelatin, or food coloring, or strawberry flavoring; whatever you want it to be, all you have to do is put it in the mold and wait for it to conform.

Most of us have done the same thing at one time or another. Who we are and how we are becomes dependent on who is around us, where we are, what situation we are in, or what is happening around us. When these things become more compelling than following Christ's example, we end up being conformed. In this world, it is definitely easier to follow the crowd than it is to follow Jesus, but worship is the very act of following Him and not choosing the easy way. This is the *take up your cross daily* part of choosing to be a living sacrifice.

It will not be forever; this world is not forever. Jesus is forever, and He says, "Do not love the world nor the things in the world. If anyone loves the world, the love of the Father is not in him. For all that is in the world, the lust of the flesh and the lust of the eyes and the boastful pride of life, is not from the Father, but is from the world. The world is passing away and *also* its lusts; but the one who does the will of God continues to *live* forever" (1 John 2:15-17). Are you prepared to choose to love the Father rather than the world that is going to pass away?

When we act as the world, going after the things of the world and living like those who are all about the world, we end up with nothing left for Jesus. The love of God is not in us, or it is spent. A living sacrifice spends it all on Jesus, reserving nothing. If we say that we love Jesus and that we follow Him, and we say we are believers, then we cannot hide our light within the world's darkness or tangle it up with the world's dark deeds and evil intentions. We must be separate from the world, because *who we are*, our lives, our actions, our speech, is our light, and our light illuminates. Is your light shining brightly in the darkness of this world or is it being dimmed by it?

The world can be convincing. Even Peter had moments when he might have stood up in the waiting room when he heard the beeping. Matthew 14:22-36 finds Paul in a boat on the Sea of Galilee. This was one of those moments. It is very late, and it is still very dark, the wee hours of the morning. The disciples have been battling storms throughout the night, and they have only managed to get as far as the middle of the sea. They are tired and weary, bunched together for warmth, and perhaps one of them is using another's shoulder to rest their head. Suddenly, through the wind and waves, the haze and the early morning horizon, they see a figure walking towards them on top of the water. Are they dreaming? Just as it would us, panic strikes the group on the boat. Verse 26 tells us about that moment of panic: "When the disciples saw Him walking on the sea, they were terrified, and said, 'It is a ghost!' And they cried out in fear."

They were exhausted and fearful. Terrified, they began screaming. The word used is *ekraxan*, which means to cry out inarticulately from a moment of deep emotion. For Peter and those in the boat with him, the emotion was terror and fear, but then Jesus speaks, and they are stunned into silence. It turns out that it is not a monster, a demon, or a ghost as they at first believed, but their rabbi, their teacher who they love.

This is Peter's moment. "Peter responded and said to him, 'Lord, if it is You, command me to come to You on the water'" (v. 28). "And He said, 'Come!'" (v. 29). While the others sat stunned and fearful on the deck of the boat, Peter broke the mold. He stopped standing and sitting at the sound of the beeping. Peter stepped out in faith, and as he did, he felt the rush of wind raking through his hair, the spray of the sea biting at his skin, and strong waves rising up and crashing all around him. As all this was happening around him, Peter saw his miracle unfold and he felt the sea tickle the soles of his feet as he walked on the water.

Some who are familiar with these passages hold the next moment against Peter. They focus on Peter sinking into the sea and forget that Peter *walked on water.* I love how Bible teacher and theologian J. Vernon McGee addresses this myopic view, writing "I hear people say that Peter failed to walk on the water, but that is not the way my Bible reads. My Bible says Peter walked on the water to go to Jesus. This is not failure!"[11]

By stepping out of conformity, by breaking the mold, Peter claimed a beautiful moment of faith, growth, reward, and blessing. He not only walked on water, he walked on water in the direction of Jesus—just Peter and his Lord, eye to eye walking on the waves. Can you imagine that moment?

In today's world, the focus seems to be on acceptance; everyone wants to fit in. No one wants to be an original or to stand out from the crowd in any way. People do not wear skinny jeans because they like them, they wear them because everyone else wears them. People tattoo their face, pierce their eyes, nose, cheeks, lips, and chest, and although they often say it is a statement of their individuality, it appears to be more likely that it is an act of garnering acceptance and establishing belonging among those in their group.

---

[11] J. Vernon McGee, *Thru the Bible with J. Vernon McGee*, vol. 4, *Matthew-Romans.* (Nashville, TN: Thomas Nelson, 1983), 85.

As believers, when Paul exhorts us not to conform to the world, what he is telling us is that we are not to put ourselves into the mold of those who live for the world. We are admonished not to pattern ourselves after the world, not to dress, talk, or act as the world does. We should not be desperate to be shaped by the world's mold, we should be desperate to be shaped into the image of God.

God wants to be the one shaping us, developing us, changing us. Jesus is the example. God wants our lives to be unique in relationship to the ways of the world, and to serve as examples of Him and His ways. Peter says we should feel like strangers, foreigners, aliens to this world. "Beloved, I urge you as aliens and strangers to abstain from fleshly lusts which wage war against the soul" (1 Peter 2:11). In this passage, Peter is identifying that the language of the world is not our language, neither is the appearance of the world our appearance. How others respond to their circumstances and context is not how believers respond.

In salmon, God gave us an example of this *counter to culture* approach. As a means of conserving energy, nearly all species of fish use the water's current to carry them along as they swim, and they move about in groups called schools to both save energy and provide safety. As the fish move they all move in unison; none of the fish would suddenly break from the group's ways.

Salmon are different. This particular fish swims against the current, and it lives its life apart from the groupings of other fish species. The sole purpose of a salmon's life is to give life. It does this by swimming long distances against the force of the water's current in order to to get to the place where it is to lay its eggs. For other fish species, their purpose is to simply exist.

Not so for salmon. On their upstream journey, these fish face jagged rocks, raging waters, fishermen, wolves, and bears, all so they can bring the opportunity for life to others like them.

Our lives are in some ways similar to the salmon. We, too, are here to bring the opportunity for life to others like us, and how we live is different from the ways of others. Like the salmon, we face dangers. Ours are not usually raging waters and bears, but they can be just as deadly. In this life, believers face dangers daily—temptation, sin, wrong moves, bad choices, and regular life challenges like sickness, violence, and the death of those we love.

For some of us, difficulties may come when a friend or family member becomes sick, injured, or dies, or when we or someone we love is ostrasized by others, is diagnosed with cancer, or facing financial ruin. Whatever they may be, it is safe to say that our own jagged rocks, wolves, and bears *will* come. Even so, we will each need to swim on. Our life is an essential upstream swim against the current, living as foreigners in this world, resisting the pull to conform, choosing instead to break the mold.

While those of the world are living for themselves, it is tempting to go the easy way—living just to survive. It is easier to blend in, not do anything that makes us stand out. This often feels like the safer option, and certainly we are much less likely to be made fun of or marginalized by the crowd. Stepping out is a choice, and much of the time it is not the easy one.

Consider Peter's moment. If he had stayed seated comfortably in the boat, if he had stuck with the group, he never would have stepped over the side and onto the water. If Peter had taken the easy way, he would have missed out on being part of a miracle. He would have lost the opportunity for his faith to be grown both by stepping out and crying out to God as he sank.

There is a lot of discussion about how Peter lost faith and began sinking. Yes, it is true that he lost heart as the storm raged around him, but he also recognized that he was in need and that Jesus was the one who could save him. Yes, he did begin to sink while the winds whipped and the waves crashed, but do not forget that he was out there! While the other eleven men were in the boat holding onto each other for dear life saying, "I'm not going in there," Peter broke the mold and stepped over the side of the boat and onto the water.

It is one thing to see a storm from the deck of a stout ship, another to see it in the midst of the waves" (It's another thing to feel the wetness from the crash of a wave hit your feet). Peter was actually beginning to sink (katapontizesqai) to plunge down into the sea, 'although a fisherman and a good swimmer" (Bengel). It was a dramatic moment that wrung from Peter the cry: "Lord, save me" (Kurie, swson me), and do it quickly the aorist means. He could walk on the water till he saw the wind whirl the water round him.[12]

Like Peter, we can walk on water. We do not have to stand and sit at the sound of beeping. We can swim against the water's current. If we shake off the paralysis that comes with fear and uncertainty, we can be transformed by God's word, walk by the Spirit, and grow in Christ. We need to reject the temptation to cling to comfort and instead embrace growth. We must walk out to where the only thing we can grab onto is Christ.

---

[12] A.T. Robertson, *Word Pictures in the New Testament*, vol. 1, *Matthew–Mark* (Nashville, TN: Broadman,1930), 119.

Peter's story is not one of failure. Yes, he began to sink, but that is part of what makes his story one of faith and growth. He stepped out in faith to get closer to Jesus, and though it was turbulent and scary he fixed his eyes on the Lord and walked toward Christ. As he got closer, he took his eyes off Jesus and began to sink, but this only grew his faith as he cried out and was saved. Because of Christ, Peter's experience was all miracle, and despite Peter's weakness, he did not fail.

The beautiful part of Peter's story is that Jesus reached down and lifted him up. That is the beauty in our own story, too. Even as the storms rage, the winds howl, and the waves rise up and crash around us with a thunderous roar, Jesus pulls us up. We may be frightened in the moment, but then, Jesus.

Peter did not behave as a follower. He held nothing back, stepping out onto the water and walking toward Jesus. No job, no relationships, no worldly ties could stop him from getting out of that boat and following Christ. It was when he stopped focusing on Jesus and started focusing on his fears that his weakness threatened to pull him under. Wisely, Peter called out to the One who could lift him up, the One who can save.

Let's face facts. When we stop conforming to the ways of the world, we pay a price. We must give up our worldly security and comfort as we stand in a vast ocean with deafening winds howling in our ears, the explosion of waves crashing all around us, and our boat too far away to climb back aboard. To come away from the crowd and step out of the boat does come at a cost, but to trust in Jesus and to follow Him is priceless. In Christ, we receive what we could never pay for ourselves.

When we make this decision, it becomes just us and Jesus working together, one to one, with our eyes locked on Him, step by step. Climbing out of our boat and onto the water means relinquishing our boat altogether. It means leaving behind whatever was in our boat—comfort, security, belonging, success, whatever we had been treasuring before our relationship with Jesus. This stepping out in faith is a rejection of everything that was hindering us from growing and from following Christ, anything that was stopping us from breaking the mold of this world. Luke writes, "And He was saying to *them* all, 'If anyone wants to come after Me, he must deny himself, take up his cross daily, and follow Me. For whoever wants to save his life will lose it, but whoever loses his life for My sake, this is the one who will save it. For what good does it do a person if he gains the whole world, but loses or forfeits himself?'" (Luke 9:23-25).

Why does it seem so much easier to follow the crowd than to follow Jesus? Following the crowd in this world is simply to be carried along like flotsam[13] on the ocean, but to follow Jesus requires us to take action. We may be fearful, we may stumble, we may even sink, but we must set our focus on Who we follow and get out of the boat. Following Jesus is taking our lives one day at a time.

What Paul relates in the remainder of Romans 12 explains what it means to live counter to the culture, and while what he writes was relevant for the culture at the time, it is just as relevant for the culture of our world today. Things have not changed as much as we may want to believe. Then and now, living in contrast to the culture has less to do with others and more to do with Jesus. It is living with less focus on ourselves and more on love, with less rationalization of the world and more worship of God.

---

[13] Floating trash or debris.

Luke reminds us that this choice, to fit into the mold of the world or break the mold and follow Christ, is a daily decision (Luke 9:23). No one lives out a lifetime of relationship with Jesus having made the decision to follow Him only once. Sometimes we have to choose again and again throughout the day, or even moment by moment.

People often talk about love at first sight, and while this type of love experience may include early attraction and kindness, love in the form of an ongoing relationship happens over time. The hallmark of this type of love relationship is a deep connection that develops from shared experience. It grows and becomes stronger over time, and is only deepened by struggle.

It is in this type of love that we present ourselves as a living and holy sacrifice to God, not a *one and done* decision, but an ongoing presentation. It is a choice we make, over and over again, to lay ourselves down and to love Jesus more than we desire the acceptance of the world. How will you choose to live?

We could choose to follow along with the school of fish, the same look, the same speech, the same discontent, just swimming along trying not to be swallowed. Or, we could choose to brave the current, dodge the rocks, and elude the bears and wolves in order to bring the opportunity for life to others like us. We could choose to settle into the mold, taking on whatever is the shape of the context we happen to find ourselves in. Or, we can choose to be this sacrifice that is acceptable to the King.

As we near the end of our consideration of these verses in Romans 12, we find ourselves at a crossroads. We are just beginning to scratch the surface, to arrive at the moment of decision. Which road will you take?

Chapter Seven

HISTOGENESIS

...but be transformed by the renewing of your mind,...
(Romans 12:2)

Have you ever considered the function of a caterpillar? They are worm-like little creatures that have only one objective, to eat. They eat and they eat and they eat, all to amass enough energy and fat stores to build a cocoon so they can undergo that marvelous metamorphosis and become what they are really meant to be, a butterfly.

While I have been aware of this process of transformation for many years, I am amazed by it to this day. That a worm bearing two compound single lens eyes, a mouth, six legs and four prolegs (that are really not legs but graspers) can enter a cocoon, liquefy into a black goo of digestive fluids and be created anew to an entirely new being is worthy of awe.

This spectacular transformation is the result of a biological process called histogenesis. Once the caterpillar is recreated, it breaks free from its cocoon to reveal itself as a completely different creature—a butterfly with four wings, six long legs, a straw-like mouth called a proboscis, antennae that serve as ears, and thousands of lenses for eyes. It is completely new, but this new creature would have never been realized without the little caterpillar's fervent and relentless focus on its one purpose.

But let's pause for a second. Go back to that biology term, *histogenesis*. This word is actually a combination of two Greek words, *histos* (ἱστός) and *genesis* (γένεσις). *Histos* from the Greek term *histémi* meaning "to make" and *genesis* meaning "beginning, birth, or life." Put these two together and it is "to make life," and that certainly defines this little bug's life. From caterpillar to butterfly, he is made new, recreated again into something new and completely different, but this renewal is not just for caterpillars. God calls us to the same rebirth in Romans 12:2. He wants to be the one shaping us, developing us, changing us, transforming us. God wants us to allow Him to make us new, and if we allow Him, he makes us so new that we are unrecognizable from our original state. Like the caterpillar, we can go from an ugly wormy existance to a beautiful new life. God is into the business of *histogenesis*.

From our rebirth we become consumers of God's word, we concern ourselves with being busy about His work, our focus becomes worship, and bit by bit our existance becomes a thing of beauty. Paul assures us that once we are reborn in Christ, we no longer are that old person, but are altogether new, and he explains, "Therefore if anyone is in Christ, *he is* a new creature; the old things passed away; behold, new things have come" (2 Corinthians 5:17).

Verse 2 of Romans 12 begins by stating two imperatives for believers who have offered their life to God's service: (1) Do not be conformed, and (2) Renew your mind. Offering or surrendering our self to God establishes a new way of living. We learn that there is something that should be shunned and something that should be done.

The world seeks to pressure us into its mold, to conform us to group thinking, collective opinion, worldly standards, wild speculation, baseless hopes, unacheiveable aims, selfish impulses, and unattainable aspirations, all of which pressure us from every direction. Be conformed *suschématizó* (συσχηματίζω) is a passive verb indicating that conforming, or being put into a pattern or mask, is something we allow to be done to us. The fact that the verb is imperative states that we are commanded to not let that happen. This word describes how living for the world means falling into line with the world, or putting on a mask to appear to fit in the world.

Paul is clear that we are not to capitulate to these pressures, but rather we are to live in the world without being like the world. This is a crucial distinction because the world wants to control how we are and how we live, but it is God who transforms us and directs our thinking. He establishes our standards and is the foundation of our hope. This is not always easy.

Consider Paul's words which offer a directive that is applied to the transformation of our daily lives.

> But you did not learn Christ in this way, if indeed you have heard Him and have been taught in Him, just as truth is in Jesus, that, in reference to your former manner of life, you lay aside the old self, which is being corrupted in accordance with the lusts of deceit, and that you be renewed in the spirit of your mind, and put on the new self, which ᶜin *the likeness of* God has been created in righteousness and holiness of the truth (Ephesians 4:20-24).

How does God renew our mind? How can we clean our brains of the corruption and garbage in there? It's straightforward, God transforms our mind and makes us spiritually minded by His word. As you listen to God's word, meditate on it, memorize it, God's Spirit renews the mind, and the lifestyle is not conformed but transformed. This renewed mind allows us to see ourselves, others, and the world from the perspective of Jesus Christ and His cross, which will replace our delight in our sins with a hatred for them, and instead of rejecting sinners, we will have a love for them.

We are to allow the transforming word of God to work within us and produce outward results instead of permitting external pressures to conform us to the world to shape us. If we meditate on God's word daily, it will influence our thoughts and help us grow more like Jesus daily. This term "transform" is a present tense imperative passive verb. We are to continually let the word of God be working in us and through us to transform us daily. It is the transforming word of God working within us that produces outward change and enables us to break the mold the world tries to keep us in.

The words "transform" and "renew" are verbs. They require action! They tell us that we cannot sit around waiting, that in order for change to occur we must participate. Think back to the ongoing work of the caterpillar whose participation was to eat continuously in order to sustain the growth required to turn it into a new and beautiful creature. Imagine him, munching and munching as he stores up the sustenance he needs, perhaps looking ahead to the butterfly he would become.

Like the caterpillar, we need sustenance for our growth. When we meditate on God's word, it influences our thoughts and helps us to become more like Jesus every day. This is why it is imperative that we come to His word daily for our sustenance, and that we allow His work to be done in us as we anticipate the new and beautiful creature we will become.

Despite the exhortations to take actions that bring about change, many Christians do nothing. They ignore the call to participate. They neither live the truth of God's word nor do the munch, munch, munching of gathering sustenance from it. These idle Christians remain still, and they are:

Still complaining
Still angry
Still hating
Still insecure
Still struggling
Still not growing
Still not praising
Still not reading the word
Still not showing His love
Still not reaching others for Christ

They are still inactive, motionlessness, because they are still not transforming. We are each called to keep renewing, keep transforming, and to abandon the "stills" and become active in our relationship with Jesus!

What do we need to change in order to be continually transformed? We need to break out of the mold that traps us in sin, let the old pass away, leave behind the old wormy caterpillar to live in the new life that is ours in Christ, to be free. We take hold of our thoughts, speech, and actions.

In Colossians, Paul teaches us about our thoughts, writing, "See to it that no one takes you captive through philosophy and empty deception, according to the tradition of men, according to the elementary principles of the world, rather than according to Christ" (2:8).   Paul uses the Greek word *philosofia* (φιλοσοφία) (the combination of the two words *philo* – –"love of a friend" and *68ophia*—"wisdom") which means "the love of wisdom" to point out the downfall of putting human wisdom before or above God's. As we are renewed, we must distance ourselves from secular wisdom, insulate ourselves from our friends' suggestions and the advice of television talk shows, and wean ourselves from the self-help messages and books that tell us to find everything we need within ourselves. Paul admonishes us to follow the truth, which is what Christ teaches through the Bible.

In addition to directing our thoughts, Paul also advises us to watch our speech, writing in Colossians 4:6, "Your speech *must* always *be* with grace, as *though* seasoned with salt, so that you will know how you should respond to each person." He is calling us to speak kindly, avoid gossip, and to do away with cursing and harsh joking. When our speech is like salt, it preserves and enhances. In this form, believers are kind and gracious toward others, specifically toward unbelievers. In this context, Paul is referring to everyday conversation and interaction. As believers, we should be recognizable by our speech.

Our actions should be to the glory of God. Matthew calls this our light, writing, "Your light must shine before people in such a way that they may see your good works, and glorify your Father who is in heaven" (Matthew 5:16). Remove the selfish actions and act for Christ!

Our light should show Christ to others. God's word offers us an illustration of this when Jesus calls four of His disciples to change their mindset from fishermen to fishers *of* men. "And Jesus said to them, 'Follow Me, and I will make you become fishers of men '" (Mark 1:17).

It takes commitment to emulate someone. I remember when my kids were smaller, they loved to dress up in Star Wars outfits. Elijah would dress like Yoda and do a little impersonation, Naomi dressed as Princess Leia and Isaiah as Anakin Skywalker. They would run around the house quoting movie lines and shooting at stormtroopers that were only there in their imaginations. On one particular day, they were having a good time doing this when I heard a whack followed by a cry.

Apparently, Isaiah got too into character and turned to the "darkside" hitting Elijah with his lightsaber. When questioned, Isaiah told me that Anakin and Yoda are enemies, and that is why he had to do that to Elijah. Needless to say, he broke character when I became Darth Vader! But wow, what commitment to the character, what commitment to becoming Anakin. The kids dressed, spoke, and acted like the people they were emulating. And if we think of it, isn't this the same type of commitment Jesus is calling for when we are asked to transform our minds?

I never wanted to be a pastor. I never liked public speaking or standing in front of crowds. I liked working with my hands. I grew up doing construction and electrical work. I pictured myself staying in the shadows, either swinging a hammer or doing wiring in a car. I never dreamed that the Lord would have me stand before people and share His message of the gospel. "The mind of man plans his way, But the LORD directs his steps" (Proverbs 16:9).

None of our plans matter when we come into relationship with Jesus! When we meet our Savior He changes us, and it does not matter where we have been or who we used to be. When we let go of whatever we were holding onto for dear life, and we follow Him, He uses us. He uses all of us, our faults and our failures, our successes and our triumphs!

We have our plans, but Jesus calls us each to His plan, just as He called His disciples.

> Now as *Jesus* was walking by the Sea of Galilee, He saw two brothers, Simon, who was called Peter, and his brother Andrew, casting a net into the sea; for they were fishermen. And He said to them, "Follow Me, and I will make you fishers of people." Immediately they left their nets and followed Him. Going on from there He saw two other brothers, James the *son* of Zebedee, and his brother John, in the boat with their father Zebedee, mending their nets; and He called them. Immediately they left the boat and their father, and followed Him (Matthew 4:19-22).

Have you ever wondered what these first disciples were thinking in those moments?—what their plans for themselves might have been?

Perhaps Peter and Andrew were planning to catch enough fish to feed themselves and their families, and have a little leftover to sell.

What about John and James? Their plan may have been about fixing what was broken, mending the nets so they would not have to spend money on new ones. Likely it was about keeping things going long enough to fish another day. They were living in a routine and in the mindset of maintaining that routine, but then came Jesus, and their thinking was transformed.

In that moment, something happened to these two pairs of brothers that stopped them in their tracks and brought their plans to a screeching halt. They met Jesus! "And He said to them, 'Follow Me, and I will make you fishers of men'" (Matthew 4:19). In that moment their plans were changed. Their entire outlook on life was changed. He called out a new pattern of thinking and new commitment of character—one that acts, thinks and talks like Jesus. He called Peter and Andrew to lay down their nets, and abandon their thoughts of catching enough, He called John and James and asked them to give up their thoughts of making it another day. . . Jesus called them to take what they knew and use it for His Kingdom. He called these outcasts, who were far removed from the upper class, to be fishers of men, to be first class followers of the King!

You may be thinking that this is all well and good for Andrew, James, John, and Peter—after all, they were apostles. And you may ask yourself, how could I, just regular everyday me, ever be in the same league with them? Keep in mind that they, too, were at times reluctant to follow, were reluctant to be changed, and just as we often do, they resisted.

> Now it happened that while the crowd was pressing around Him and listening to the word of God, He was standing by the lake of Gennesaret; and He saw two boats lying at the edge of the lake; but the fishermen had gotten out of them and were washing their nets. And He got into one of the boats, which was Simon's, and asked him to put out a little distance from the land. And He sat down and *continued* teaching the crowds from the boat. Now when

He had finished speaking, He said to Simon, "Put out into the deep water and let down your nets for a catch." Simon responded and said, "Master, we worked hard all night and caught nothing, but I will do as You say *and* let down the nets." And when they had done this, they caught a great quantity of fish, and their nets *began* to tear; so they signaled to their partners in the other boat to come and help them. And they came and filled both of the boats, to the point that they were sinking. But when Simon Peter saw *this*, he fell down at Jesus' knees, saying, "Go away from me, Lord, for I am a sinful man!" For amazement had seized him and all his companions because of the catch of fish which they had taken; and likewise also *were* James and John, sons of Zebedee, who were partners with Simon. And Jesus said to Simon, "Do not fear; from now on you will be catching men." When they had brought their boats to land, they left everything and followed Him (Luke 5:1-11).

What we need to remember is that even in their resistance, Jesus sought out Andrew, James, John, and Peter, and He does the same for you and for me.

These men were exhausted from a long hard day that left them with nothing to show for it. Then, Jesus, a carpenter by trade, comes along telling these fishermen how to do their work. Peter was well aware that the time for catching fish had passed for the day, but he humors this carpenter anyway. Consider the manner in which Peter responds to Jesus' instruction. If we read between the lines we can imagine it in today's language: "Hey, Mr. Carpenter, I do this for a living, and I know how this works. We have already done all we can do, but fine, let's do it."

Immediately, Jesus provided Peter with a huge catch, nets teeming with fish. With such a great catch of fish ready for market, Jesus calls Peter again, "Follow me." This time Peter understands, he leaves his earthly treasures and comforts to follow Jesus.

Jesus' call to Peter is to break the mold of his *do what it takes to survive* thinking, and instead turn his thoughts to Him. It is a shift from survival to living beyond survival, to living daily with purpose, with the purpose of being made more like Christ.

"They forsook all and followed him – They had followed him before, [see] John 1:43, but not so as to forsake all."[14] At first they clung to their regular lives. Although they followed, they hadn't rejected everything and they had not made the decision to follow Jesus whatever the cost.

They followed, but when it became uncomfortable, they reverted to following their old ways. When they got hungry they followed their bellies. When they had no money they followed their income-producing work. When they got tired they followed their pillows. At first they fell into the mold of the world, but ultimately they realized what Jesus was calling them to do, to follow Him and to change their thinking from being fishermen (survival), to being fishers of men (Christ-like). It was then that they left their old life behind to follow Jesus.

To follow means to take guidance and instruction from someone. It is a total commitment, and it is without hesitation or excuse. Peter's old life made him the right choice to be a fisher of men as Jesus wanted him to be because he was a stubborn, rough around the edges, and passionate everyday man (Acts

---

[14] John Wesley, "*Wesley's Explanatory Notes.*" Bible Study Tools, (1754–1765), http:www.biblestudytools.com/commentaries/wesleys-explanatory-notes/luke-9.html (accessed July 10, 2011).

4:13). As Peter denied himself to follow Him (Luke 9:23), Jesus saw Peter as the perfect vessel to bring Him glory.

It did not matter then and it does not matter now what is our education level or what is our physical appearance, or any other worldly measure of value, importance, or influence. What matters is that we are willing to leave our comfort zone, to leave our pride, to leave our desires, to leave it all and follow Jesus.

Jesus' desire is that each of us would abandon the excuse that we are not right for the job, that we would stop telling ourselves and by extension telling Him, "I cannot, because I am just ordinary." By understanding that ordinary is extraordinary in the eyes of Jesus, each of us can begin to view our life through His lens, and we can each begin to see that we are equipped by Christ to be fishers of men.

As we stop patterning ourselves in the mold of the world, we cease talking, dressing, and acting like the rest of the world. Jesus desires that each of us would break the mold of what the world tells us we are, and see ourselves through His eyes. He wants us each to be a person that sees every encounter, every opportunity, every task, every moment as having eternal significance, to be a person who seeks after His own heart in all things. It is this perspective, this view, that breaks the mold, and which best reflects the renewing of our minds that embodies our transformation (Romans 12:2).

We are not to conform to the mold of other people or to the mold of society and culture, because God wants to be the one to mold us, develop us, change us, and in the words of Romans 12:2, transform us. God wants each of our lives to be unique examples for His glory, and for each of us He has already given so very much.

Throughout the human history recorded in the Bible, there are only two occasions when a father was faced with sacrificing his son. The first of the two is Abraham. This father was tested to see if he loved his son, Isaac, more than he loved God; he did not. As Abraham raised the knife to drive it into his only son, God stopped him and Isaac was spared.

The second is God Himself and His Son, Jesus, who He did not spare. God's sacrifice is a testament to the fact that He loves each of us so much that He allowed His only Son to be nailed to a cross, to bleed, and to die, all to demonstrate His great love for us.

Now it is our turn. It is time for each of us to crawl onto the altar and lay ourselves down to show our love for Him. It is time to show that we love Him above flesh, family, work, money, and things. It is time for us to be changed from a selfish sinner into a child of God. It is time to be becoming daily more Christ-like. It is time to change our minds, change our actions, change our lives, and live for His glory. Allow God to rearrange your life. Allow Him to start the *histogenesis* of transforming your life, your mind, your speech, and your actions.

Chapter Eight

REMAIN IN HIS WILL

... so that you may prove what the will of God is,...
(Romans 12:2)

I have heard couples that have been married a long, long time say the key or trick to a long marriage is staying in love! I have thought about this and wrestled with this over the years. Today, after two decades of marriage, I finally grasp what those couples were sharing. The idea of staying in love is often associated with cards, flowers, or chocolates. It has also been tied to the physical attraction of love, the feeling of having butterflies. However, the key is not butterflies or gift giving. The key is staying in the love you have. That is how you stay in love.

The true key to staying in love is to love as you have been loved, and to stay in the love given to you. Jesus says,

> "If you abide in Me, and My words abide in you, ask whatever you wish, and it will be done for you. My Father is glorified by this, that you bear much fruit, and so prove to be My disciples. Just as the Father has loved Me, I have also loved you; abide in My love. If you keep My commandments, you will abide in My love; just as I have kept My Father's commandments and abide in His love. These things I have spoken to you so that My joy may be in you, and that your joy may be made full (John 15:7-11).

The way to stay in love with God is not to stay in love with Jesus, but to stay in Jesus' love!!! It does not say love Me more, or love my word more or love one another more. The passage says remain, stay in, be in, don't leave my love.

Long ago, in the days before cell phones and home computers were common, when the Internet was accessed by dial up and we all used manual printers called typewriters, I remember my brother attempting to have a long distance relationship with a neighbor's niece in Canada. In those days, international phone calls were prohibitably expensive and email was not common enough to be an option. So, my brother and his girlfriend had no way to be in communication and express their mutual love other than the now old-fashioned postal letters affectionately known as "snail mail."

I recall one weekend he was telling all his buddies about his amazing girlfriend, but little did he know that the letter was already in the mail. It had not arrived yet, but the news that she had broken up with him was on its way. It probably should not have surprised any of us. With no in person conversation, no hand holding, no shared experiences, and nothing more tethering than a hand written letter to sustain it, their youthful love was destined to fail.

My brother's relationship failed to grow roots because he and his girlfriend were too far away from one another, they were not able to know each other deeply, and they simply were not in touch regularly. The same is true for many believers; they are in a long distance relationship with Jesus. They are not in personal contact through prayer and study, and they are not living shared experiences with Jesus by their choices and lifestyle.

How do we end our long distance relationship with the Savior? John 15:7 makes it clear. The way to a thriving, personal relationship with Jesus is to abide in Him, and to allow His word to abide in us. In this verse, Jesus directs "abide in Me," and the Greek word used is *meinéte* (μεἰνητε), meaning "to continue to be present." Jesus is telling us that we need to be present, to stay close, to abide.

How do we remain present with and stay close to Jesus? Jesus provides the answers Himself. In John 15 He says, "I am the true vine, and My Father is the vinedresser. Every branch in Me that does not bear fruit, He takes away; and every *branch* that bears fruit, He prunes it so that it may bear more fruit" (vv. 1-2). When Jesus talks of the struggling branch that is not fruiting, in the English *"takes away"* is a poor translation. The word Jesus used was *aírei* (airei) and it means "to lift up," "to pick up." It's the same word Jesus says about taking up your cross to follow Him in Luke 9 and in Matthew 11 when He says give me your burden and take mine because it's easy to carry and light to bear. It's a holding up, a lifting, it's a distribution of weight! It's where we get the word air from!

And God seeing you being dragged in the dirt by life and sin wants to lift you up. But in order for this miracle of growth toward the Son to take place, we need to learn what it means to be in a relationship. We need to appreciate what we have and nurture it!

John's account of Jesus' words continues:

You are already clean because of the word which I have spoken to you. Remain in Me, and I in you. Just as the branch cannot bear fruit of itself but must remain in the vine, so neither *can* you unless you remain in Me. I am the vine, you are the branches; the one who remains in Me, and I in him bears much fruit, for apart from Me you can do nothing. If anyone does not remain in Me, he is thrown away like a branch and dries up; and they gather them and throw them into the fire, and they are burned (John 15:3-6).

Keep in mind the relationship of the vine and branches. Some branches stand up, growing toward the sun, giving fruit and enjoying life in the vine. But there are others which stay at the bottom, separating themselves from the growth up top, from giving the weight of burden to the vine, and they are at risk of separating and drying up!

There was a time when I grew black raspberry vines, and I remember the vine dressing that had to be done. Winter meant hours spent cutting back and carefully pruning the branches. It was time-consuming work, definitely not easy work, but by the time Spring arrived the branches would begin to flourish, and by Summer they would be laden with berries. Interestingly enough, as the harvest of fruit commenced, I forgot the hard work I had done with the branches. I was excited and happy to harvest the sweet fruit, and I remember thinking that it was well worth the effort I had put in during the early days.

The work did not end there, though. During summer, as the branches grew, they had a tendency to get too long and weighed down and they would sag into the dirt. I would have to keep tying the branches to sticks, poles, and lattice to keep them from rooting directly into the dirt. If I did not continue to care for them, they would no longer draw their sustenance from the large, thick roots of the vine that had sustained them. Instead, they would attempt to rely on their own small, superficial root newly dipped into the dirt. If the branches were left to fend for themselves instead of relying on the vine, they would perish. The branches were always trying to establish their own roots in the superficial connection to the earth, but they could not survive that way. The life of the branches was inexorably tied to the vine.

This is not a warning of losing salvation. This is not a warning of being sent to Hell. This is a warning of losing the relationship with your Savior. Stay into the source of that salvation and into the source of that growth. If you separate yourself from love for the dirt of the world you will grow harsh and brittle to what the Lord offers you! We become like the dried wood of those self-rooted branches. When He tries to reach us the relationship has grown cold and been cut off. Though He tries to feed us, our dried up souls do not absorb His sustenance.

If this sounds familiar, be encouraged. Jesus does not give up on us. He keeps trying. He continues to do a trimming of the dead parts in the life of every believer. Anyone who has ever kept fruit plants knows that regular trimming is essential because it helps the branches produce more fruit.

When all the unnecessary bits and pieces are removed, there is no longer valuable energy being spent on useless endeavors. Therefore, all of the branch's strength is directed toward the purpose—to bring forth fruit. Being pruned is a good thing for the branches because they no longer need to waste their energy on the superficial leafy growth that produces nothing, and falls off with the first hint of a breeze.

Friends, when we chase after things that will not last, when we put our focus on temporal comforts and selfish desires, we waste our fruit-bearing energy and we lose sight of our divine purpose, which is to glorify God with our lives. If we focus on popularity, acceptance, money, status, and material things, we have only superficial leafy growth that is swept away by the slightest wind. These useless bits and pieces sap our energy, weigh us down, and leave us fruitless.

> Now if any man builds on the foundation with gold, silver, precious stones, wood, hay, straw, each man's work will become evident; for the day will show it because it is to be revealed with fire, and the fire itself will test the quality of each man's work. If any man's work which he has built on it remains, he will receive a reward. If any man's work is burned up, he will suffer loss; but he himself will be saved, yet so as through fire (1 Corinthians 3:12-15).

How do we thrive? We stay in love. We stay in love with the One who loves us. We stay where we are cared for, where we are nourished and pruned so we can bear fruit and fulfill our purpose. We stay in the relationship that matters, because Jesus is there waiting for us. We stay in His love.

The story of the prodigal son is a parable of the Father's love. The prodigal son takes his worldly possessions and goes off to immerse himself in the filth and decay of the world. Why was he susceptible? Why did he suffer? Because he separated from his father's love. The good news is that all he had to do to be restored to his position as the beloved child was to come back, to engage once again with the love of his father. In that moment, he was once again drenched and immersed in love. This is God's love for us.

What causes relationships to fail and families to crumble is the belief that there is another love, a better love, somewhere else, somewhere out there. This is not Jesus' approach to relationships in the family of God. He says, "Just as the Father has loved Me, I also have loved you; remain in My love" (John

15:9). He invites us to stay, and tells us just how to do that. Not only this, He offers Himself as our example, "If you keep My commandments, you will abide in My love; just as I have kept My Father's commandments and abide in His love (John 15:10). Jesus is telling us that if we abide in His love, meaning if we stay where we are and immerse ourselves in His word, if we read it, experience it, sing of it, and pray about it, we keep the love going. We pass it on.

There are four actions that help us to stay put in the love of Jesus, four things to do that keep the bond of love strong. The first is to read His word. When Jesus says, "If you remain in Me, and My words remain in you," (John 15:7a), we can see that we are to let His word saturate our lives and be reflected in our lifestyle. We abide in Jesus' love by reading and knowing His word. David said, "Your word I have hidden in my heart so I will not sin against you" (Psalm 119:11). God's word not only shows us where we go wrong, it also guides us to focus on what is right, on God's love for us, and to bear in mind always how His love was demonstrated on the cross at Calvary.

When we are staying in the love of Jesus we are not only reading and knowing God's word, but living by it. We are to use God's word to guide us in wisdom and understanding, to use the Bible as a navigation tool, as instruction in times of confusion or indecision. The psalmist recognized this when he wrote, "Your word is a lamp to my feet And a light to my path" (Psalm 119:105).

We do not have to figure everything out on our own, however. We have a role model, an example in all things. We need only ask ourselves, what would Jesus do? The Bible is God's own word, provided for our edification and for our maturing in our relationship with Jesus, As believers, we should seek it, in fact crave it; "and like newborn babies, long for the pure milk of the word, so that by it you may grow in respect to salvation," (1 Peter 2:2). When we allow the word to abide in us, we can grow, be guided, and gain wisdom.

The second action is to ask and receive by praying in His name. John 15:7 states, "ask whatever you wish, and it will be done for you." This is the promise to us that we need only ask. We simply need to bring our petition to Jesus. To have the love of God stay with us or abide with us we need to be praying. We must put our petitions before the Lord in prayer, and also believe that our prayers are answered. Jesus Himself tells us, "Therefore, I say to you, all things for which you pray and ask, believe that you have received them, and they will be *granted* to you" (Mark 11:24). When you pray believe that God is able to do what you pray for.

At the same time, we cannot expect to call on God as if He were an automated dial in number. It is not as if we call in and simply press 1 for blessings, 2 for reassurance, 3 for forgiveness, 4 for strength, and 5 for healing. The expectations of this world can lead us to think that when we ask God we should hear an immediate response, or at least hear an automated voice saying, "You are the 110th asker, your prayer is important to us. Please, stay on the line, and it will be approximately 219 minutes before your ask is answered."

This hold message may be acceptable when seeking plumbing assistance, or waiting for your insurance agent, but Jesus says, we should not call the answering service. He says, "Contact me directly, call My cell, send Me a text, My phone is always on, I am always listening." "And whatever you ask in My name, this I will do, so that the Father may be glorified in the

Son. If you ask Me anything in My name, I will do *it* " (John 14:13-14).

In addition to reading and learning His word, and asking in faith in the name of Jesus, the third action is to be fruitful. Our purpose is to glorify the Father, bringing forth praise from our mouths, and from the mouths of others—this is our fruit. "My Father is glorified by this, that you bear much fruit, and so prove to be My disciples" (John 15:8). The fruit we bear proves we are His disciples. It means we have learned from Him and live   for   Him.

When someone plants a mango seed they do it with the intention of growing mangoes. No one plants a mango seed expecting it to bear cauliflower; that would be a big disappointment. No, when we plant a mango we are expecting to enjoy mango fruit from it. We expect the green-red skin of a mango, the bright yellow flesh of a mango, the sweet, delicious smell of a mango, and the juicy, mouthwatering taste of a mango.

In Christ Jesus it is just the same. Because we are in His tree, in His family, He expects that we would bear the same type of fruit He does. "But the fruit of the Spirit is love, joy, peace, patience, kindness, goodness, faithfulness, gentleness, self-control; against such things there is no law" (Galatians 5:22-23). This is a list of spiritual gifts that identifies the recognizable characteristics of our spiritual fruit. Our fruit is related to Jesus, and we are therefore recognizable in the same way that the taste, sight, texture, and smell of mango is differentiated from that of cauliflower. As Christians, our lives should be easily differentiated.

When God sees our lives He knows what family we belong to, and in the same way, when others see us as part of God's family, they want to be part of it, too. Why do they want to have what we have? Because they watch how we live. Our lives are not without trials or challenges, but it is how we live out those moments or seasons that make us different.

Others see for themselves that our lives are linked to our family of God. They may think, "he is so kind," or "she is such a joy," or "they are such giving people." They may wonder how we find peace in challenging circumstances as we hold to our faith in the trials of this life. It is in our circumstances that we are bearing fruit, when people see who we are and how we live. It is then that others think, "I'll have whatever they are having."

It is our lives, our actions, and our willingness to share the work God has done in our lives that is our testimony. This is how we witness to unbelievers and invite them to receive the good news of the gospel. Through our lives the Holy Spirit draws people to salvation in Christ. The Holy Spirit is at work through us, but our job is only to plant seeds, to open our mouths and convey the good of God that has transformed us.

The fourth action is to live according to the commands of Jesus. But, do not confuse this with the Law of Moses. In John 15:10 Jesus states, "If you keep My commandments, you will abide in My love; just as I have kept My Father's commandments and abide in His love."

So what are Jesus' commands?

A new commandment I give to you, that you love one another, even as I have loved you, that you also love one another (John 13:34).

Do not be amazed that I said [or commanded], "You must be born again" (John 3:7).

This is My commandment, that you love one another, just as I have loved you (John 15:12).

Jesus' commands are: (1) trust Him for salvation, (2) stay in His love, (3) love the family of God and (4) love others! This is how we remain settled in the love of Jesus, how we stay in love with Him, and how we keep falling in love with Him over and over again. And the beauty of it all is that when we fall head over heels for Jesus through these four areas there is a promise for our life at the end of the passage in John 15. Read the entire passage again.

> If you abide in Me, and My words abide in you, ask whatever you wish, and it will be done for you. My Father is glorified by this, that you bear much fruit, and so prove to be My disciples. Just as the Father has loved Me, I have also loved you; abide in My love. If you keep My commandments, you will abide in My love; just as I have kept My Father's commandments and abide in His love. These things I have spoken to you so that My joy may be in you, and that your joy may be made full (John 15:7-11).

Now, let's zero in on verse 8, "and so prove to be My disciples." They say, "proof is in the pudding". This is an old saying to get people to try foods they wouldn't normally try because of its look. Pudding looks gross, but when one tries it, their opinion changes. Proof that it is good comes from trying. I think for the believer we should say, "proof is in the putting," because we need to be putting God's word into action, our faith into action and our lives into action. We prove to be followers of Jesus by abiding in the word, praying and bearing fruit and none of those can take place if we are not being transformed by the word of God and applying it and acting on it!

God's word is the means by which His will is conveyed in our lives. It is how He communicates His plan for all the areas of our lives and this world. And believers are taught to actively seek to do His will, live His will, and pray for His will. "Pray, then, in this way: 'Our Father, who is in heaven, Hallowed be Your name. Your kingdom come. Your will be done, On earth as it is in heaven'" (Matthew 6:9-10). When prayed by believers, this prayer is a statement of faith, and a commitment that for as long as it takes until we are present with Him, we will live for Him.

I love going to visit my parents in Titusville. We spend hours rocking on the porch, drinking coffee, and talking. However, even as we do, my mom is not sitting still; she is always in motion. She does not allow a moment to be wasted. Earlier I shared that my mom is someone who cleans, I mean *really* cleans. In her world, if it does not smell like bleach, it is not clean. We can be talking late at night and she will be wiping the kitchen counter as she chats. When we are getting ready to leave for church, she has every chair on top of the dining table as she mops. You just cannot keep my mama from her cleaning! She is never idle, always using the moments in between to accomplish something good.

This is the mentality we are called to have as believers. As long as we are waiting, we can do some cleaning. As long as we are awaiting Christ's return, we can use the time in between to do some cleaning in our lives. We can scrub away wrong living and live according to God's word. We can sweep away the dirt of lust and covetousness, to live a life of service to God. And, we can rub away our guilt, anger, and bitterness, and polish it into forgiveness, love, and mercy. "For to me, to live is Christ and to die is gain. But if I am to live on in the flesh, this will mean fruitful labor for me; and I do not know which to choose" (Philippians 1:21-22).

We look forward to being in the presence of Jesus with excited anticipation, but while we are waiting, we are to be useful and productive with our lives. So our prayer needs to be if I must wait for that time of freedom, Lord, then let freedom and grace be lived in my life. Let me work for your kingdom here on earth. Let me be your ambassador to the kingdom that will not pass away. When Paul said he was an ambassador in Ephesians 6:20, he was saying that he was the foreigner, speaking and living in a foreign land on behalf of his King. When I speak it is for Him, when I work, live, and how I act speaks for Him and His kingdom. In other words, I am living God's will on earth. I am living for Him.

To pray this prayer with any meaning in our lives, with any impact in the words, we should find out, what is a will? *Thelema*, in the Greek, means "a request, desire or wish, something one wants." In essence, what you are saying in Matthew 6:10 is, "God, what you want done, let it happen on earth, just like in heaven. What you want happens".

For us, this means that in every circumstance we should be looking for opportunities to impact the kingdom of Christ. After all, this is the prayer we offer to the Father, "Your kingdom come" (Matthew 6:10). His kingdom will come, this we know by faith. So, in the meantime, our lives are to work for His kingdom here on earth, to be an ambassador for His kingdom that will never pass away.

This is a prayer request to the believers of Ephesus, "and *pray* on my behalf, that utterance may be given to me in the opening of my mouth, to make known with boldness the mystery of the gospel, for which I am an ambassador in chains; that in *proclaiming* it I may speak boldly, as I ought to speak" (Ephesians 6:19-20).

In other words, Paul is saying that he is happily in bondage for his work on behalf of Jesus. In fact, his concern is not for his chains at all but that he would not be timid or reserved. He asked for prayers that he would be courageous to speak plainly and boldly about the gospel.

Paul makes the point that he is living God's will on earth, living for Him alone, answering His call and doing His wishes, not as a slave or servant but as God's own delegate to the lost. Paul is a blueprint for our labor, and from his example we can model our own actions. Just as my mom is always in motion to keep a clean house, we need to be looking for every opportunity to be useful and productive for His kingdom, even as we wait.

In essence, the prayer Jesus teaches us in Matthew 6:10 is like today's believers saying, "God whatever You want done, let that happen on the earth, just the way that whatever You want is just what happens in heaven." In order to pray this prayer authentically, with meaning and impact for our lives, we should understand that the Greek word found in this verse is *thelēma* (θέλημα); this is a desire. This is important, because it means that our prayer is that we would be actively participating in the will of God in our lives. This prayer asks that the desire of God Himself would come to pass in this world, just as God's desires are joyfully fulfilled by the angels in heaven.

Of course, God's will is not always easy, and that is true whether the one doing His will is human or angelic. For example, in Daniel 10, God sent an angel to deliver a message to Daniel, but the angel was waylaid by a demon army for twenty-one days; the angel describes, "But the prince of the kingdom of Persia was standing in my way for twenty-one days; then behold, Michael, one of the chief princes, came to help me, for I had been left there with the kings of Persia" (v. 13).

Doing God's will on earth is sometimes hard, and as we read in Daniel 10, it can be challenging for angels as well. It is important to note that even when an army of demons gets involved, angels find a way to get God's will done because they want to get it done. We have to want to get God's will done, too. We have to want it badly enough to make a way. Like the angels, we have to want to do it, and when you truly want to do something, it gets done.

So, what do we do? To make the path of life more comfortable to walk, God left a blueprint for us in His word. We are beloved, and God does not want any one of us to be lost. His desire is that each and every one of us would believe on Jesus and the fact that He died for us, and therefore we would be saved. Peter tells us that God is "not willing for any to perish, but for all to come to repentance" (2 Peter 3:9).

What is God's will for our lives? As we read in Romans 12:2, "And do not be conformed to this world, but be transformed by the renewing of your mind, so that you may ᵈprove what the will of God is, that which is good and acceptable and perfect." The will of God is that you be transformed by His word and not conformed to the world.

Are we trying to please God and do His will in our lives even when we fall short? "For the sorrow that is according to *the will of* God produces a repentance without regret, *leading* to salvation, but the sorrow of the world produces death" (2 Corinthians 7:10). God desires that we would feel the pain of sin and ask forgiveness, He desires us to reject the wrong living they are doing and embrace salvation. God's desire is that we would repent and thereby not be condemned to the hopeless sorrow of the world, which is death.

Despite the challenges and struggles, are we living to do what God desires of us? Ephesians 6:5-6 tells us that we are to be vigilant, obedient, and living rightly, not as a show for others but because we are willingly and joyfully serving Jesus "not by way of eyeservice, as men-pleasers, but as slaves of Christ, doing the will of God from the heart" (v. 6).

In 1 Thessalonians we find several directives about God's will for our lives. In 4:3, God's will is that we would "abstain from sexual immorality." God desires that we remain sexually pure. In 5:18 God's will calls for us to be always thankful. His desire is that we would "in everything give thanks" no matter the circumstances. His will is that we would be glad in all things.

First Peter also gives us insight into God's will for us. Peter writes, "For ᵃsuch is the will of God that by doing right you may silence the ignorance of foolish men" (2:15). It is God's will for us that we would not fight back against unbelievers and those who would hate us because of Jesus. Instead, it is His desire that it would be by the quality of our living which is the illustration of our transformation, that unbelievers and others would have nothing more to say.

To understand where we are at in our own walk with Jesus, we have to answer some hard questions. And, the answers are for each of us as an individual follower of Christ.

- How am I *really* doing?
- Have I been living to fulfill God's will in my life or am I just living for my own desire?
- Do I live out what I want rather than what God wants of and for me?

- Am I striving to show I belong to Christ, and am I reflecting Him through my actions and choices?
- Am I saying, "Lord, while I have breath or until the trumpet sounds, I am living for you"?

By His grace and the power of the Holy Spirit, Jesus reveals and enacts God's will, and through Christ we are all invited to know God's will. As believers, we are drawn into it and enabled to live by it. Jesus says, "For whoever does the will of God, this is My brother, and sister, and mother" (Mark 3:35).

Chapter Nine

DOING GOD'S WILL

"that which is good and acceptable and perfect." (Romans 12:2)

In this portion of the text, we find a descriptor of God's will. God's will is good. Have you ever used the phrase, "Lord willing" or "God willing"? What do people mean when they say that? What do *you* mean when you say it? Do you go out of your way to make sure the Lord's will happens in the situation and in your life? The truth is many people do not want God's will in their life. If they did, they would be acting it out, they would be living it, and they would be trying it. Instead, people want their will. But the Bible tells us we should be praying for God's will, which implies that we are asking for help to implement it. "Your kingdom come. Your will be done, On earth as it is in heaven" (Matthew 6:10).

The phrase your kingdom come is something we say but sometimes don't dwell on the meaning of. What is the kingdom of Christ? We find an answer in 1 Corinthians 15.

Then comes the end, when He hands over the kingdom to the God and Father, when He has abolished all rule and all authority and power. For He must reign until

> He has put all His enemies under His feet. The last enemy that will be abolished is death. For HE HAS PUT ALL THINGS IN SUBJECTION UNDER HIS FEET. But when He says, "All things are put in subjection," it is evident that He is excepted who put all things in subjection to Him. When all things are subjected to Him, then the Son Himself also will be subjected to the One who subjected all things to Him, so that God may be all in all. (1 Corinthians 15:24-28).

The kingdom of Christ is the rule of Christ on David's throne with His people for a thousand years, when He limits the curse of the land, where the lion and the lamb will come together.

> Then I saw thrones, and they sat on them, and judgment was given to them. And *I saw* the souls of those who had been beheaded because of their testimony of Jesus and because of the word of God, and those who had not worshiped the beast or his image, and had not received the mark on their foreheads and on their hands; and they came to life and reigned with Christ for a thousand years. The rest of the dead did not come to life until the thousand years were completed. This is the first resurrection. Blessed and holy is the one who has a part in the first resurrection; over these the second death has no power, but they will be priests of God and of Christ, and will reign with Him for a thousand years (Revelation 20:4-6).

When we pray for the kingdom, we are praying for the one that defeated sin, and death to sit on the throne of David in Jerusalem. The prophecy of Isaiah 11 will take place where the line of David, the root of Jesse will rule righteously (vv. 1-5). The lion and the calf will graze together, and the wolf and the lamb will sleep together (vv. 6-7), because there is no predator and prey. And the baby will play with venomous snakes with no fear of being bit (v.8). Isaiah 2:4 says the ground will be very fertile with no weeds or thorns, dryness or sand, that people will turn their weapons into farming equipment, and for the milenia, there will be no demons, no devil, no wars, and a limited curse on the land! This is what every believer must pray for. This is what we must long for and anticipate. It should be what we are longing for. Scripture says the earth longs for it and grumbles for it.

> For the eagerly awaiting creation waits for the revealing of the sons *and daughters* of God. For the creation was subjected to futility, not willingly, but because of Him who subjected *it*, in hope that the creation itself also will be set free from its slavery to corruption into the freedom of the glory of the children of God. For we know that the whole creation groans and suffers the pains of childbirth together until now. And not only *that*, but also we ourselves, having the first fruits of the Spirit, even we ourselves groan within ourselves, waiting eagerly for *our* adoption as sons *and daughters*, the redemption of our body (Romans 8:19-23).

Please Lord free us from corruption and sin, remove the evil around us, the pain, disease, and cancer.

During Jesus' reign, this world will see God's plan unfold the way it was originally meant to occur in the garden. However, we are not yet at that day. So, in the meantime, until the day we are either breathing our last or we are in the moment when we "will be caught up together with them in the clouds to meet the Lord" (1 Thessolonians 4:17), we have a job to fulfill.

That job is implied in the prayer Jesus taught us: "Your kingdom come, Your will be done" (Matthew 6:10). We are to be doing His will. Lord, we await that time in joyous anticipation, even so, in the meantime, we want to be doing Your will.

Scripture is clear that the saints will rule at His return. Consider these examples:

- "If we endure, we will also reign with Him; If we deny Him, He will also deny us" (2 Timothy 2:12).

- "And he said to him, 'Well done, good slave; since you have been faithful in a very little thing, you are to have authority over ten cities.' The second one came, saying, 'Your mina, master, has made five minas.' And he said to him also, 'And you are to be over five cities'" (Luke 19:17-19).

- "You have made them *into* a kingdom and priests to our God, and they will reign upon the earth" (Revelation 5:10).

- "But the court will convene *for judgment*, and his dominion will be taken away, annihilated and destroyed forever. Then the sovereignty, the dominion, and the greatness of *all* the kingdoms under the whole heaven will be given to the people of the saints of the Highest One; His kingdom *will be* an everlasting kingdom, and all the empires will serve and obey Him" (Daniel 7:26-27).

- "Does any one of you, when he has a case against his neighbor, dare to go to law before the unrighteous and not before the saints? Or do you not know that the saints will judge the world? If the world is judged by you, are you not competent to *form* the smallest law courts? Do you not know that we will judge angels? How much more matters of this life?" (1 Corinthians 6:1-3).
- "And if you belong to Christ, then you are Abraham's descendants, heirs according to promise" (Galatians 3:29).
- "and if children, heirs also, heirs of God and fellow heirs with Christ, if indeed we suffer with *Him* so that we may also be glorified with *Him*" (Romans 8:17).

The reigning is reserved for those of us who remain faithful in the waiting. We MUST pay attention to the idea of reward. Scripture tells us to. "And without faith it is impossible to please Him, for he who comes to God must believe that He is and that He is a rewarder of those who seek Him" (Hebrews 11:6).

It is essential that we do not lose sight of the fact that our entrance to heaven is a gift, not a reward. We did not earn it. In fact, we could never earn it. Despite the overwhelming cost to Jesus, it is completely free to us.

His will be done. How do we live for Jesus in our waiting? We stay busy! Like the servant in the parable of the talents in Matthew 25, we need to be busy about our Master's business, with our goal being to one day hear those precious words: "Well done, good and faithful slave. You were faithful with a few things, I will put you in charge of many things; enter into the joy of your master" (v. 23).

And, what does busy look like? Matthew 6:10 gives us valuable insights. If we must wait for that time of freedom, we can have freedom and grace be lived in our lives in the meantime. We can simply ask Jesus, "Lord, let me work for your kingdom here on earth, let me be your ambassador to the kingdom that will not pass away." When Paul said he was an ambassador in Ephesians 6:20, he was saying I am the foreigner speaking and living on a foreign land on behalf of my King. When I speak it is for Him, when I work, live and how I act speaks for Him and His kingdom. In other words, I am living God's will on earth. I am living for Him, how He requests and doing His wishes, as his delegate to the lost.

We begin by putting our trust in Jesus and accept our position as His child. When we allow Jesus to work in us, let His love and grace shine through us, we are living His will. When our salvation takes over and makes transformational change infectious, we are living His will. Doing God's will is not earning salvation, it is allowing God to work through us so His kingdom can be seen here on earth; "for it is God who is at work in you, both to desire and to work for *His* good pleasure" (Philippians 2:13).

Living God's will can be difficult at times. However, as an ambassador of His kingdom, we enjoy a very special relationship with Him. Mark relates an occasion when amid a crowd, someone announced that Jesus' family members were looking for Him. Jesus' response gives us clarity on the special nature of our relationship with Him. In Mark 3 we read that instead of going off to find his mother and brothers, Jesus used the moment to teach the crowd about the relationship He has with believers. Verses 33-35 read, "Answering them, He *said, 'Who are My mother and My brothers?' Looking about at those who were sitting around Him, He *said, 'Behold My mother and My brothers! For whoever does the will of God, he is My brother and sister and mother.' "

In this passage, Jesus does not focus on attachments to those that were physically related, but instead identifies that what matters is those who are spiritually related to Him, His family members are His followers. This is especially important as we remember that Jesus' mother did not travel with the twelve as they went about sharing the good news of grace, and Jesus' brothers did not spend time seeking and saving the lost!

In fact, in John 7 we read, "For not even His brothers were believing in Him" (v. 5). When Jesus went about hiding from the Temple Guards and Priests as He performed miracles in small cities, His brothers told Him not to hide, but to make Himself known out in public. Had Jesus followed their direction, He would have been arrested, but Jesus knew it was not time, and He had much left to do.

He knew what his brothers were thinking, and "So Jesus said to them, 'My time is not yet here, but your time is always opportune'" (v. 6). His earthly family had not come into spiritual relationship with Jesus yet. They were disconnected. While they were family in the flesh, they were not yet brothers with Christ in the Father's love.

We are brothers, sisters, and mothers in the family of Jesus. We are His followers who call Him Savior, who demonstrate Him to others, and who live rightly and joyfully no matter our circumstances. This is our special purpose within the family, and God wants us to stay focused!

Mark 3:35 makes the definition of Jesus' family unquestionable, because Jesus Himself states, "For whoever does the will of God, he is My brother and sister and mother." Jesus is stating categorically that His family is made up of the ones working with Him to accomplish what the Father sent Him here to do. Our Father sets the agenda, and Jesus says that His family are those that work with Him to that end. In other words, Dad makes the plan for us, and together as a family we get it done.

And what was the agenda the Father set? What was the divine purpose Jesus was sent to fulfill? "For the Son of Man has come to seek and to save that which was lost" (Luke 19:10). The purpose of Jesus on earth was to seek and to save, and our purpose is very much the same. We are here to find the lost and share the love of the Father with them. Our goal is to come alongside the outcast, the downtrodden, and those who recognize their need for a savior, and to share the love and forgiveness we ourselves have already received.

Our purpose is to tell others that they, too, can live and not die. If any one of us had a friend standing too close to the edge of a cliff, we would certainly tell them how unsafe it was, but it is a fair bet that most of us would not stop with that warning. Most of us would also earnestly urge them to move back from the danger, to take a step in the right direction so they would live and not die. What good would it do to sit back and wait for a person to figure it out for themselves without any help while they risked death in every moment?

In Luke 19:10, Jesus uses the verbs *seek* and *save*. The actions belong to Jesus. He is doing the seeking and the saving. He is not waiting for the lost to find Him. There is no action the lost need to take in order to to be sought and saved. Jesus is active in His duty and busy at the agenda God set forth for Him.

Just as the disciples of the Bible were busy seeking and saving, as followers of Christ, we need to be busy with our work for God's kingdom, too. The disciples did not sit back idly waiting for the lost to arrive to them. They worked their mission. They labored at their role. They did not wait around. They took the plan and ran with it.

Jesus had been going from place to place performing many signs and wonders. John 5 and John 6 relate the experience of Jesus' sermon on the mount. People were following Jesus in a growing crowd. In John 6:1-13, one of His longest sermons, He spent hours teaching a crowd of people numbering in the tens of thousands. When it was late and everyone was very hungry, to the amazement of His disciples, Jesus fed them all with just five loaves and two fishes.

Jesus' ministry boomed. People were following Him in droves, and the talk of the town was Jesus the Teacher. You could say that Jesus had the first megachurch. You could also say that He was the first pastor asked to leave the pulpit. Jesus' message, His plan, His vision, was not the power statement the people wanted.

The people wanted a King that would overthrow Rome, unseat Herod, and stop the corruption among the religious leaders. They wanted power and might, not love and forgiveness. In John 6 His followers cry out, asking Jesus to lead them, be their Moses, rescue them from the Romans and Herod who were their Egypt. They wanted Jesus to overcome their oppressors. But Jesus' answer was not what the people wanted to hear and the numbers following Him dwindled. "As a result of this many of His disciples withdrew and were not walking with Him anymore" (v. 66).

While there had been 10,000 or more in the crowd, this number soon reduced to 72, and then from that 72, only the 12 remained. But the twelve understood. "So Jesus said to the twelve, "You do not want to leave also, do you?" Simon Peter answered Him, "Lord, to whom shall we go? You have words of eternal life" (vv. 67-68).

The crowds withdrew because His plan was not popular enough, the goal was not majestic enough, and the people thought their ideas were better than God's agenda. But Jesus was about the Father's work, and He was about accomplishing what *God* asked of Him, not the what the people clamored about.

> For I have come down from heaven, not to do My own will, but the will of Him who sent Me. And this is the will of Him who sent Me, that of everything that He has given Me I will lose nothing, but will raise it up on the last day. For this is the will of My Father, that everyone who sees the Son and believes in Him will have eternal life, and I Myself will raise him up on the last day (John 6:38-40).

The will of God was, and is, to reach the lost, to bring life to them through the work Jesus did on the cross. Yet, for the crowds in Jesus' time, this purpose just did not deliver on their expectations. And so, Jesus went from megachurch (10,000+), to small church (72), to a home church (12 disciples).

While some may interpret this as some kind of collapse or decline, the fact is that Jesus' home church of twelve disciples shared with Him a common goal, and this made them family. "And extending His hand toward His disciples, He said, 'Behold: My mother and My brothers!'" (Matthew 12:49).

There is a key part of the passage pointing to some of Jesus' blood family coming with opposite goals. Mark 3:32 uses the Greek, *zētousin* (ζητοῦσιν), which means "inquiring of" or "searching for" in this verse. Jesus' relatives of the flesh were seeking the Seeker, while his spiritual family were out seeking according to the will of the Father. This can be said for us about our relatives and our family.

Who is our family? While many of us would immediately think of relatives in the group we were born into or grew up in, this verse in Mark 3 encourages deeper consideration of this question: "For whoever does the will of God, this is My brother, and sister, and mother"' (v. 35). We have an earthly family that is deserving of our attention, care, and concern. This is underscored by Jesus who cared deeply for these relationships in His own life. Relatives of the flesh are important to Jesus, and should be to us, too.

However, we also have a spiritual family whose connection to us far exceeds the limits and boundaries of this life. This family is defined by Christ Himself as being those that do the will of God to seek and save the lost, those who live in this purpose. Family extends beyond flesh and blood to include the eternal purpose for which we are all created. "Therefore if there is any encouragement in Christ, if there is any consolation of love, if there is any fellowship of the Spirit, if any affection and compassion, make my joy complete by being of the same mind, maintaining the same love, united in spirit, intent on one purpose" (Philippians 2:1-2).

We come together as family, by the Father, in the Spirit, and through the Son. We become family when we are transformed, made new as like-minded followers who live for the will of God that His kingdom, indeed, would come. This is family.

How do we live out our transformation? How do we live with the family goals in mind? It is not complicated.

Pray. We pray as Jesus did, "yet not My will, but Yours be done" (Luke 22:42b). Pray that His will would be done here on earth, that He would make us bold and give us opportunities to participate in Jesus' *seek and save* mission.

Reach Out. When we are transformed and living in the will of God, we are actively looking for the lost all around us. We remain alert and watching in the same way that Jesus and His twelve brothers were seeking the lost in all situations and circumstances. (Remember Paul, imprisoned, in chains, but still praying to be bold and courageous for the lost around him? [see Ephesians 6:19-20])

Do. If we only think or talk about taking action in the will of God, we are not living along with the family. We need to use the boldness and courage that is ours in Christ to have conversations, to hand out flyers, cards, and tracts, to invite people to church, to share the gospel and the transformation that we ourselves have experienced.

Ask. Jesus said, "Therefore, I say to you, all things for which you pray and ask, believe that you have received them, and they will be *granted* to you" (Mark 11:24). So we ask, already knowing that He will answer us. Ask the Lord to build the church, to guide the leaders, to establish a ministry, to grow faith, and as many contemporary songs and writings suggest, to break our hearts for what breaks His own. Ask Him, and then trust Him with the answer.

Yield. When we give over to God what we have been trying to do on our own, and we give up trying to force God into our myopic plans, we yield our will to His. When we finally let go, we are freed from the constraints of our own limitations. We must yield to Him at work, at home, in our relationships, while we are watching TV, driving to our appointments, waiting in line at the grocery, and in all other situations and circumstances.

Yield, and watch Him use us for the glory of God and the coming of His kingdom.

Now that we have been made new creations, we have the opportunity to model to the world what it means to be transformed. We can demonstrate a life lived for Jesus, according to His word. We can reveal what it means to put our thoughts, intentions, and actions under subjection to Him, and what it means to live in God's will. We can show how our circumstances are no longer the determinant of our joy, and as living sacrifices, we can testify to the freedom that comes from our salvation!

Chapter Ten

THE DECISION

Therefore I urge you, brethren, by the mercies of God, to present your bodies as a living and holy sacrifice, acceptable to God, *which* is your spiritual service of worship. And do not be conformed to this world, but be transformed by the renewing of your mind, so that you may prove what the will of God is, that which is good and acceptable and perfect (Romans 12:1-2).

Having worked our way through Romans 12:2, you are now facing a decision. Are you a butterfly transformed from the old worm crawling along the ground into a new and beautiful creation? Or, are you gelatin that reshapes and adjusts itself into whatever mold the world wants of you?

If we are transformed and made new, when we read the Bible, hear a sermon, or have something else stir us or convict us, we are spurred to action by these experiences. However, if something presses on our hearts and we do not respond with the action we are called to, we are being deceived. When we hear what we should do or understand how we should act, but we remain unchanged, we are deluded.

Are you in the same place you were before we began this journey? It is my prayer that you are seeing things differently after our journey together. Ask yourself: Will I allow God to transform me, or will I walk away from this experience unchanged? I earnestly pray that it is clear to you what we as believers need to be doing and how we are to go about doing it according to the word of God, but only you and God can know for certain.

> Therefore, putting aside all filthiness and all that remains of wickedness, in humility receive the word implanted, which is able to save your souls. But prove yourselves doers of the word, and not merely hearers who delude themselves. For if anyone is a hearer of the word and not a doer, he is like a man who looks at his natural face in a mirror ; for once he has looked at himself and gone away, he has immediately forgotten what kind of person he was. But one who looks intently at the perfect law, the law of liberty, and abides by it, not having become a forgetful hearer but an effectual doer, this man will be blessed in what he does. (James 1:21-25).

As we have discovered together in Romans 12:2, Paul is begging us to give ourselves to Jesus, to give over all that we have and all that we are, our whole self, holding nothing back. Becoming a living sacrifice is something we do in thankfulness for the mercy God has shown us. Mercy is the gift of not getting what we deserve. As sinners, we deserve punishment for the bad things we do, but instead, our merciful God gives us what we do not deserve. This is the grace of God.

There are blessings in store for those that seek the Lord, who commit themselves to live by His word and grow in Jesus Christ. "Blessed is the person who does not walk in the counsel of the wicked, Nor stand in the path of sinners, Nor sit in the seat of scoffers!" (Psalm 1:1). The person who seeks the Lord does not follow the lead of unbelievers or comply with the ways of the world. Instead, the person who follows Jesus takes advice from God's word, and is guided by what the Lord has to say about their trials, their joys, and whatever their circumstances are.

Conversely, a wicked person walks with wicked people, their inner circles are wicked, their thinking is wicked, and their actions are wicked. Some may recoil at the word wicked, but we can easily exchange if for worldly or selfish. The Hebrew word for wickedness is *rishah* (רִשְׁעָה), but this Hebrew word is also used to mean guilt or moral wrong.

Whichever word we use, ultimately, what the passage is saying is that we are not to get advice from self-interested people or live our lives in the manner of unbelievers. A transformed person stands clear from the one always thinking of themselves and their gain, and does not walk their path.

Amos 3:3 asks, "Do two people walk together unless they have agreed to meet?" This verse points out that by walking together we have a common understanding. We are going the same way. The path of the wicked is painful, hurtful, and lonely. The one who rejects this path is blessed, as translated from the Hebrew word *esher* (אֶשֶׁר) meaning "happiness." When we surround ourselves with like-minded followers of Jesus, we rest easy as we avoid the dangerous advice of self-serving people.

When we let God's word take root in our lives, it grows. As His word directs our lives, it makes us productive for His kingdom. Psalm 1:2 says, "But his delight is in the law of the Lord, And in His law he meditates day and night." Delight in and meditate on God's word. This word, delight, from the Hebrew word *chephets* (חֵפֶץ), means "desire" or "good pleasure." We become content and rest in pleasure when we have found our place in God's word. When our walk is a walk with the Lord, when we seek His word as our path, when we live for His will and His kingdom, then we find contentment. And, our happiness is no longer dependent on the circumstances of this life.

Psalm 1:2 gives us insight into from where our happiness, our relaxed contentment, comes. By rejecting incoming advice, rejecting association with wicked people and the direction of unbelievers, we can bear fruit. We can live always in blossom because we take in God's word, and we live by it.

When we open our hearts to the Lord, He provides fertile soil for our growth, and we receive watering from the well of Jesus. We never suffer drought or hunger. As the word of God takes root in us, we are perpetually refreshed and strengthened, always looking for opportunities to seek and save for the glory of God. "He will be like a tree planted by streams of water, Which yields its fruit in its season, And its leaf does not wither; And in whatever he does, he prospers" (Psalm 1:3).

This the life that awaits us when we refuse the way of the wicked and choose instead the path of the Lord. No longer traipsing around in our sinful ways, but walking in peace and fulfilling the purpose we share with Jesus and our spiritual family. Of course, we must actually do the walking along the path of the Lord, but when we do, we avoid the pits of selfishness and sin. "But I say, walk by the Spirit, and you will not carry out the desire of the flesh (Galatians 5:16).

This is not unlike what we read in Amos 3:3 and Psalm 1. The person that loves the Lord, who loves and applies His word, out of that person comes the goodness that they themselves have received through Jesus. When we are firmly planted, the hard times do not shake us, the storms in life do not blow us off course, our faith stands strong because we know the truth of God's word is unchanging. When comes drought, sickness, pain, suffering, even death, when others fall away, we still believe because we are rooted in the vine Himself. It is to Him that we look and are strengthened and comforted.

As followers of Christ, we know hard times come, but we know, too, that God still loves us and the answer is to turn our eyes upon Jesus. We recognize that there will be pain and sorrow, but we know that Jesus died for us, and we live in His glory and grace. We know that contentment and happiness result from being attached to the vine. We read and meditate on the truth that is the word of the Lord, because His word will never fail us. And, as members of the family of Christ, we know our purpose is to tell a dying world of His perfect salvation!

The same cannot be said for the wicked. Scripture tells us, "The wicked are not so, But they are like chaff which the wind blows away. Therefore the wicked will not stand in the judgment, Nor sinners in the assembly of the righteous. For the Lord knows the way of the righteous, But the way of the wicked will perish" (Psalm 1:4-6). These who are not rooted in God's word, the branches who are not drawing their life from the vine, these are not walking in step with the Spirit. They are like chaff, blown here and there as tumble weeds in the wind. They have no root in God's word, and they are not trying to grow and be fruitful.

To live a meaningful life is to be living God's word, to be rooted in Christ and transformed into a new creation that lives in God's will. Meaning in this life is found in Christ. It is found in being a family that shares a single purpose, to seek and to save with every opportunity. Psalm 1:2 tells us to delight (study God's word) and meditate (seek to understand and apply it).

It is time to stop conforming to the world, time to break the mold of the world. Living like gelatin that strives always to fit into the mold means that, in any given moment, we are defined and our lives are determined by whoever we happen to be with, whatever situation we are in at the time, where we are, whose acceptance we seek. We end up living like and for the world.

Gelatin conforms, but butterflies are transformed! Out of the ugly life of a worm they are made into a new and beautiful creature. "And do not be conformed to this world, but be transformed by the renewing of your mind, so that you may prove what the will of God is, that which is good and acceptable and perfect" (Romans 12:2). Transformation comes when we choose to change our life and our mind as we follow Jesus!

The old life was all about fitting in and twisting ourselves into whatever shape worked for the circumstances. In that life we have to be careful not to ruffle feathers, not draw attention, and we keep our focus on being accepted. The transformed life is nothing like that. God's word identifies over and over again that we are specifically called to be set apart. Peter explains who we are as new creations: "But you are a chosen people, a royal priesthood, a holy nation, a people for God's own possession, so that you may proclaim the excellencies of Him who has called you out of darkness into His marvelous light" (1 Peter 2:9). He also entreats us to live the transformed life, telling us "but like the Holy One who called you, be holy yourselves also in all your behavior; because it is written: 'You shall be holy, for I am holy'" (1 Peter 1:15-16).

Ultimately, each of us must decide for ourselves if we will lay our self down as a living sacrifice, turning from the old and embracing our transformation into a new and beautiful creation, living in the will of God, and as a member of the family of Jesus to seek every opportunity to share the gospel of salvation with a lost and hurting world.

We each have a choice whether to live in our old ways for the acceptance of the world, or to break the mold and live for Jesus in thankfulness for all He has done for us.

"knowing this, that our old self was crucified with Him, in order that our body of sin might be done away with, so that we would no longer be slaves to sin; Even so consider yourselves to be dead to sin, but alive to God in Christ Jesus" (Romans 6:6, 11).

Scripture Index

Made in the USA
Columbia, SC
13 July 2021